HOW WE WON THE WAR

OR, YA GOTTA BE KIDDIN'! YOU GOT AWAY WITH THAT?!

CHARLES G. PEFINIS

authorHOUSE®

AuthorHouse™
1663 Liberty Drive
Bloomington, IN 47403
www.authorhouse.com
Phone: 1-800-839-8640

First published by AuthorHouse   3/22/2010

ISBN: 978-1-4389-6526-0 (e)
ISBN: 978-1-4389-6524-6 (sc)

Library of Congress Control Number: 2010901868

Printed in the United States of America
Bloomington, Indiana

This book is printed on acid-free paper.

DEDICATED TO MY WIFE . . . MY LIFE
SANDRA MATHESON PEFINIS

Thru all these 56 precious, vibrant, funny, loving years (4 trying to convince her to marry me and 52 after she said yes)

Sandra has been my inspiration my love. She has heard most on my Army stories. She read them again as the editor. ***"Charles, I think you should eliminate some of these words . . . . ."*** Meaning that I should eliminate words that were crotch oriented or anal lytic, hmmm! "But my love <u>that</u> is the way we said things in the Army."

Think about it Sandra. A guy's whole life style in the service was so different from what he was accustomed to. For example, my best friends were a construction company vice president, a watch repairer, a farmer, a truck driver, a Harvard guy and a pimp!"

In some ways that is the essence of this book. It is a series of vignettes, the stories from young men from all over our nation whose life changed dramatically from that of a being a civilian to that of a killer of men whom one never knew of nor to which had any antipathy.

The Good Lord has blessed me with this incredible lady and given us a wonderful, beautiful loving family.

For this I am eternally grateful. Efxaristoe Thaey mou!

Charles G. Pefinis

THANK YOU TO THESE SPECIAL PEOPLE

First to those who gave me permission to include their stories, Thank you again! Without your personal submissions it would not have been published. Also, equal thanks for those who gave me permission to use information from their own media sources.

My thought as I contemplated doing this book, was to be a gatherer of stories that dwelled in men's minds or that they had written.

It was indeed an honor and a distinct privilege to be given this permission.

Being a novice computer guy, (I should have read, Computers for Dummies!) I did not store the material for easy access for the publisher. This necessitated all the pages being typed again. In March, I placed an ad for a typist in Craig's List. Within hours, emails began coming in, tons of them! Many volunteered to assist me in many ways. One young Marine, Julianna Graham stationed at nearby Fort Mead, Md.* requested that she be "given the privilege of typing it gratis." I was touched and very appreciative. (It must have taken her many hours.) I will be honored to pay her an appropriate amount.

Julianna, is a 27 year of mother of three. She enlisted in the Marines in 2000, went to boot camp in 2001, She has served at several stations and was recently promoted to Staff Sergeant (E-6). She plans and dreams of eventually becoming an author or journalist.

Her husband was deployed to Iraq in 2003. Though he suffers from PTSD, he is managing it well and going to school.

I was truly honored to have such an individual, a true American patriot, to assist me in this work. Thank you again Julianna!

I am not able to give attribution to those Craig List responders but here is my official "THANKS TO ALL OF YOU!

An unexpected result is the "virtual" friend ships that have evolved from the book. To those new friends, I say Thank you very much!

Charles Pefinis

Piff was my nickname in the infantry.

* I was stationed for a few days at Fort Mead in January 1945 just prior to taking the train to New York. My two sisters and mother came to see me off. They marveled at my physical condition – "bulging" muscles and my having put on weight. That rigorous "basic Army training" and that good ol' Army chow gained me 20 pounds! Who said the Army did not feed you well!

WHY I WROTE THIS DIFFERENT
BOOK ABOUT THE "GOOD WAR"

Many years have past, 65 to be exact, since my discharge from the Army in 1945. My story, my experience, probably mirrors that of many of those who served in the armed services in the World War II.

Yet strangely, my most vivid memories that persisted thru all these years in my mind (not "notes from a log") are not of horrific happenings but rather those that could be considered "normal" to an 18 year old.

Eighteen year old boys in my day, enjoyed "doing things", high school, riding cars fast, "watching the girls go by", sports, eating, dating, talking, flirting, joking about everything while standing and talking in early summer evenings at the neighborhood corner, those kinds of joyful everyday things. These kinds of things, the Army version, stuck in my mind.

The American sprit is my name for what drove us. It is an unfettered, independent, don't-give-a-damn, beat-the-system method of operating, yet all under a disciplined environment.

As I discussed my pending "book" with friends and acquaintances,my comment was, "I want those events that you experienced that were not hurtful or horrific but those that were informative, or inexplicable, inspiring, funny as hell or religious in content."

I believe that what you will read here conforms to that concept.

There is one major exception that in no way mirrored our eighteen year old civilian life. That is the selection of one's close friends in no way left up to us.

I was a combat infantryman. My best "buddies" would die for me as I would for them though I had just joined them as a replacement.

Let me describe them to you. Fran, debonair, bright, was a vice president of his father's construction company in upper New York state, Walt, absolutely brilliant from Massachusetts with a semester at Harvard, Al(for Aloysius which he despised) from Potstown, was a husband (that is all he would tell us. He dug his fox holes very deep, "cause of my kids at home"), Dave, his dad owned a trucking business in New York, Perdue from Kentucky a good-ol'-boy, very brave and down-home scary in his combat skills, Tony, from the Bronx, an "Eye-talian" Charmer, (the kind you see portrayed in a WWII movie); "Buddy" a watch repairman from Indiana and finally Carlos (combo

Spanish and something) also from New York - but Manhattan - a pimp! "Piff, (spoken in a Brooklyn accent) when its over, you come to New York. I'll fix you up with as many girls as you want, all free, courtesy of your friend, Carlos!"

The men in a squad, 10, were very close. Walt was promoted to our platoon leader, an eighteen year old, leading, controlling the lives of about 40 men. The camaraderie was palpable. All those eighteen year old civilian things described above, continued but within the crucible of war and terror. That is why the American service man became the conqueror. He was not constrained by protocol, he was a creative, independent thinking person, much to the consternation of our disciplined (but equally courageous enemy).

Many of the stories in this first book are mine. As said above, I did not keep a log or diary of my experiences. Luckily the action I saw was at the end of the Bulge. The war was ending in Europe. From my discharge thru all of these years, I do not remember clearly many horrific events. I can still hear vividly the cries of the wounded. "Medic! Medic!". The sound of a wounded soldier calling out to his Mother, "Mommy, Mommy", really unnerved me.

Yet except for the excerpts in this book, all the others I witnessed were erased from my mind. My first sight of a dead soldier, a German, was in a tiny village in Belgium. It stunned me. I saw this man laying there on his back, wearing a rather ornate grey and white uniform with epaulets, no signs of blood his eyes opened "staring" at the blue sky. As we moved toward the end of the villages' boundaries, there were two American bodies laying there on their backs with their faces covered by a GI blanket. That is the first time I saw what parts of a human brain looked like.

This book's purpose is to chronicle those happenings that were not horrific so why write those words above. My answer is to try to explain what happened to me in severe battle situations. My mind sort of "floated" above them. The reason I believe is due to a deep religious upbringing by my parents and especially my maternal grandmother which produced an aura of protection not unlike a "cloud" that encompassed my mind. I was always afraid but never hysterical. (Read: God in Combat . . .A Grandmother' Love)

So this book is a compilation of my stories and those of other Army, Air Corps, Air Force, Navy, Marine, courageous men (no Coast Guard stories yet. I hope to gather some for the second volume.) who served our magnificent Nation with honor, dignity, patriotism, and courage battling powerful enemies who sought to defeat our American way of living "with liberty and justice for all!"

Charles G. Pefinis

Contents

"HOW WE WON THE WAR…

O R,

YA GOTTA BE KIDDIN'! YOU GOT AWAY WITH THAT?!"

BY CHARLES PEFINIS

YES, THESE STORIES AND EVENTS ARE TRUE. THEY ARE MY RECOLLECTION OF WHAT I EXPERIENCED AS A SOLDIER DURING WORLD WAR II. THEY ARE NOT HORRIFIC. THEY ARE A REFLECTION OF AN 18 YEAR OLD'S ABILITY TO COPE AND LIVE THROUGH THE MOST DRAMATIC CHANGE AND EVENTS IN HIS LIFE.

THEY ARE INEXPLICABLE, INFORMATIVE, INSPIRING, HUMOROUS AND RELIGIOUS IN CONTENT.

AS A MEMBER OF "THE GREATEST GENERATION", AS TOM BROKAW REPORTS, WE SAW, BEFRIENDED, AND LIVED WITH PEOPLE OF DIFFERENT MORES, TRADITIONS, AND RELIGIONS. OUR LIVES WERE TEMPERED AND CHANGED FOREVER BY THESE EVENTS.

GRACIOUSLY, I HAVE BEEN GIVEN STORIES FROM OTHER PERSONS WHICH ARE INCLUDED. I ASK FOR SUBMISSIONS FROM ANY VETERAN FROM ANY CONFLICT FROM ANY NATION. THANK YOU.

CHARLES G. PEFINIS

AUTHOR,

"How We won The War...or, Ya Got to be kiddin'!
Ya Got Away with That?!"

Pefinis-Matheson Theme Books P.O. Box 397 Timonium, MD 21094

www.howwewonthewar.com

ANECDOTES FROM VETERANS
FROM THROUGHOUT THE WORLD
THAT ARE
AMAZING, INSPIRING, INEXPLICABLE, HUMOROUS
INFORMATIVE OR RELIGIOUS IN CONTENT

"HOW WE WON THE WAR, OR YA GOTTA BE KIDDIN'!
YOU GOT AWAY WITH THAT?!"

CHARLES G. PEFINIS, AUTHOR
PEFINIS-MATHESON THEME BOOKS
WWW.HOWWEWONTHEWAR.COM

HOW WE WON THE WAR . . . . . .A STRANGE TITLE

How We Won the War etc! is a strange title. There have been many books written about war particularly about World War II. The movie," Saving Private Ryan" was the catalyst for this book.

I saw that movie. It was a unique experience for me because attending with me were my two sons-in-law rather than my wife always my companion before this. They knew I had served in combat. That was the extent of their knowledge. They learned more.

As we drove home, the silence that prevailed gave testament to its effect upon them. They had really never given much thought to what it might have been to have served in battle and also constrained by a system, where one has no free freedom. One must conform. You must do what some real jerk - at times- tells you to do.

What this website and book hope to describe in detail is the way these people – civilians - lived and functioned as warriors. This in reality identifies and defines the American character and spirit. These attributes are what make our Nation the greatest in the world.

There are few sad references to actions or events included. As a cover page states, what we recorded are those stories that were amazing, inexplicable, humorous, informative or religious in content.

Upon your becoming a service person, you take on a different persona. You become one with your colleagues particularly those with who you are in combat. What is astounding is the mix of people, who become your "family", your buddies. Mine included a watch repairer, a truck driver, construction company vice president, a hair dresser and a pimp!

As is written in other pages, this book and others that will follow, is made of stories of real life episodes of persons that served their country in war.

Charles Pefinis

Publisher

PEARL HARBOR... I WAS THERE... A DREAM LOCATION
CONTRIBUTED BY WILLIAM MUEHLEIB

It was December 7th 1941. Our .50 caliber positions were located at about 300 yard intervals along what we called "bomb dump road." This was the access road to where the bombs and ammo were stored. Our gun positions were for 50 to 75 feet from the road. It was the afternoon after the attack and no one knew what was going on.

By this time we were hungry and thirsty and, sure enough, a GI truck with rations and canteens came cruising up the road tossing canteens and rations to us as they drove by. It was a pleasant break after all we had endured earlier.

We ate the sandwiches but went sort of light on the water, not knowing when we would get more. Well, about two hours after the ration distribution, here comes a fire truck up the road with the sirens going, scaring the hell out of us. GI's hanging on the side of the truck were yelling into amplifiers, "Don't drink the water! It's been poisoned!" Well, that was it. For the next couple of hours we just sat there waiting to feel the pain of poison, waiting to die.

We were not, though, passing out or dying. What happened (probably) was that some admiral figured that with all the Japanese living on the island, they might just have poisoned our water supply (pretty brilliant!) therefore the best way to keep the troops from drinking it was to tell them it had been poisoned.

It had not. Well, for several days after that, all of our drinking rations were in cans or bottles. If it wasn't the Japanese scaring the hell out of us, it was our own command.

Contributed by William (Bill) Muehleib, Virginia Beach, VA

THE FOLLOWING ARE MY STORIES: BY CHARLES PEFINIS

This is my hometown, Atlanta, Georgia and these are my stories. I was born there and schooled there at Tech High School, where I was in ROTC, Major of the 3rd Battalion.

This picture was taken in the late 1930's. Further North past the large tower clock—Kay Jewelers—is the haberdashery where my parents would purchase suits for my dad and me, Hertz Clothiers.

An interesting side note about Tech High ROTC: In the spring of 1943, we were honored by the visit of Carlos P. Romulo, who came by to see an old friend of his, Colonel Clarke, our MST&T (head of ROTC in the State of Georgia). They were at Corregidor, Phillipines together on General Douglas MacArthur's staff. They both escaped on the sub with MacArthur.

Colonel Clarke allowed all the cadet officers to actually meet with Mr Romulo. He was later awarded the Pulitzer Prize, for a series of articles on the Southeast Asian political situation. He was president of the UN General Assembly and also became Ambassador to the U.S.

I WENT AWOL MY FOURTH DAY IN THE ARMY

My induction day in the Army was on Monday 11-22-43 at Fort McPherson outside of Atlanta, Georgia. Thanksgiving Day was the coming Thursday. By Wednesday the place was like a morgue. Only a skeleton (no pun intended) crew of the cadre was on post. Man, we were bored to death (again, no pun, etc). There we were, a bunch of brand new, wide-eyed 18 year old, Army haircutted, nervous recruits not knowing what the hell to do except to go to the show or to the library. Not too desirable.

I called home and spoke to my mom who was the best cook in the world, especially for holiday cooking. When I hung up the phone, I was salivating. "Damn, my last time for a long time to taste Mom's delicious cooking, and here I am hung up at this damn, dead Army place. I got to get the hell outta here some way." So I went to the Sarge with a plaintive look and explained what I wanted to do, asking permission to have a two day pass. He said NO!

"Hey, wait a minute," I thought, "I'll go see Vic. He's probably going home for Thanksgiving!"

Vic was my cousin who was a typist in the typing pool at Fort Mac. Vic had a car. So this is what we did. Vic loaned me one of his Army jackets festooned with the few ribbons we all had and his corporal stripes. Man, in the Army for four days, and I am already a corporal! (For the record, I never attained this prestigious rank until a few days before I was discharged in May 1946. I never put the stripes on. I figured some day I would be acclaimed something and I would take pleasure in that the Army never knew what it had in me and my superior something. I was doing all of these wonderful things as a lowly P.F.C.)

Vic told me, "Cuz, you sit behind me; as we drive by the gate, and the guard looks at us, he is a friend. Give him a wink, and he will walk over to the window and peer in. Give him $5.00, a bill, not ones, squashed up in a ball, okay?"

Okay! Man, I am going home for Thanksgiving, 15 miles away. So, that is what we did. We got "home" before bed check, same guard, and except for a little indigestion from too much turkey, slept like a baby. What a way to start my Army service, going Absent Without Official Leave my fourth day!

PLEASE, SARGE, GIVE ME A PASS! I JUST GOT MARRIED!

I was inducted at Fort McPherson in Atlanta, Georgia. It was November of 1943 and a bunch of guys there were mostly from New York and Pennsylvania. Don't ask me how they got there; I just don't know. I really forgot this young man's name, but he was Italian and his father was a big shot with Ford Motor Company in Detroit. We will call him Tony.

Tony was devastated. He had just gotten married and he had spent only one night with his bride. She had come to Atlanta and was at a downtown hotel waiting for him. It was Thanksgiving weekend. He, too, went down to this old sarge and asked for permission to have the weekend off to spend with his young bride.

The sarge this time did let him down easily. He cited all the rules and regulations and felt that there was some compassion there and appreciation, nevertheless, it was an impossible thing for him to do.

Now, this is where the old American ingenuity took hold. By then, we knew the system of the bed count. If I remember correctly, we would all have to be in bed by, say, 11:00, and then the sergeant would walk in, go down the barracks, and look at all the bodies in bed. If every bed had a body in it, then everyone was accounted for.

I walked up to Tony and said, "Let's try a little scheme here." I got all our buddies around and came up with this method to make Tony "disappear."

We took Tony's bed apart, stashed his barracks back and all of his personal belongings in the large bathroom area, then moved all the beds sideways slightly occupying the space that Tony's bed used to have, making everything look nice and neat and perfect.

Old Sarge walks in the first night, scans all the beds and walks out and closes the lights. We did this each night for three nights. I forget how Tony managed to get in early each morning, but he sure did. We put his bed and things back each morning where it should be. Everything was perfect. Sadly, Tony was killed in Belgium in February.

MIAMI BEACH! WHAT A PLACE FOR BASIC TRAINING!

When I arrived in gorgeous Miami Beach, Florida in 1943, I was enthralled by its beauty, the verdant growth, and the beautiful hotels, so art deco with very pastel colors. It was glorious!

Three things happened to me in Miami I remember so vividly. They were somewhat unique and gave substance to the entrepreneurial spirit and creativity of the American soldier.

We had to go to the rifle range to learn how to shoot our Garand rifles. The countryside was simply glorious but the rifle range was devoid of any vegetation. You lay down with your rifle, quickly and slowly scoped the targets, and endeavored to shoot a Bulls-eye.

I do not know to this day why the target was named "Maggie's drawers" but that's what it was called. The procedure was that at times you would spell each other's duties. You'd go behind the barrier and be the Maggie's Drawers lifter up and puller downer—oops. In essence we would be the force to make these targets go up and then bring them down after the shooting session ended. Frequently spent bullets would bounce around us, not with a lot of force but sort of scary anyway.

Our second day there we were all lying together in a prone position, training our rifles on targets on Maggie's Drawers. For some reason, there was a stub of wood about ten inches high stuck in the sand. It might have been part of a sign with the sign now off. We gave it no notice. Suddenly a beautiful white bird about the size of a crow came fluttering down oblivious to the racket being caused by the guns going off. Gently and tenderly he lit upon this stub.

As if under control of a robot machine, thirty rifles immediately took aim at that poor little bird, from left, from right, from in between and from the center. Almost like a command, the shot went out. The poor little birdie disappeared in a cloud of feathers. Now in retrospect that might not be a nice thing to do, but in those days it was funny and we all howled at it.

We also got chewed out by the D.I. He had just opened his mouth to probably say "DON'T SHOOT!" but too late!

At times our squads were called on to compete with each other in various I'll-kill-you-enemy tactics—cowboys and Indians. The winner got one "Attaboy."

It was about 7:00 am one morning. We were sitting on the ground in damp but beautiful Florida listening to boring lectures by our instructors. I have a high tolerance for cold but except for Belgium February 1945, I had never been as cold in my life as being in Miami Beach in December sitting on damp sand. At times, one shook uncontrollably. We all wore long johns. I mean it. By the afternoon, we were sweating profusely. Can you imagine wearing long johns in Miami Beach, Florida?

The session for this day was to camouflage ourselves so well that the other teams could not find us. That was relatively easy because of the plentiful supply of leaves and fronds, Florida fauna.

Pete, my erstwhile friend, who was tiny, (you'll meet him again), was a sneaky devil. He had goofed off one day hiding from the Sergeant. A place suddenly dawned on him as a perfect place for our group to hide. The palmetto trees in that part of Florida grow large. They are like large fans that are coupled together, making a beautiful setting. Pete had found one where the sand had drifted away at the base—he had done some of the drifting himself—it was sort of a "tunnel" like space that one could crawl through and when you emerged you were sitting in the center—atrium –like—a nice cool spot surrounded by these beautiful fronds. It was heaven.

So, with Pete as our fearless leader, we went to his favorite palmetto tree. We dug out more sand; we could all crawl through and under the base. Then by pushing the sand back, we covered the hole. There we were, sitting all comfy and quiet in a nice area about five feet wide.

We could see everything going on around us. The teams began looking for each other and eventually all were found but our group. There was some consternation evident with our Sergeant. He remarked, "Where in the hell did those guys go? Did they go AWOL? We looked everywhere for those guys. Where in the hell did they go?"

Well, we were not more than twenty feet from them, they just could not see inside the leaves of the palmetto unless they came right up close to it. The deadline finally came and at 5:00 we emerged as the winners of the contest. Again, we snaked our way out but this time, in the reverse direction, from under the fronds to the cheers of our buddies, but to the jeers of our adversaries. The look on ol' Sergeant's face seemed to say "Hey, guys, that's not fair!" But it was, and we won.

7

Luckily, I developed a toothache in Miami Beach. We were domiciled in beautiful art deco, gorgeous, old—in those days—hotels. We were at the "Tides."

I reported my toothache to my Sergeant, who directed me to the medical people. They directed me to a dentist in Miami Beach on Collins Avenue! I was given some instructions and a notice to go to Collins Avenue, about a mile away. I'd report to this dentist and get relief from my toothache.

Now imagine this, here is an 18 year old kid, wearing Army fatigues about 10:00 in the morning, having a free pass to walk down Collins Avenue in that gorgeous city with all kinds of normal activity going on around him, people talking, beautiful girls, horns honking, lights changing, the smell of coffee— Oh, it was wonderful.

Well, old Pefinis developed a perpetual toothache. That thing "hurt" me almost every other day. To this day, I think the dentist was conniving with me without telling me. So, about four times over a period of about two weeks, I would saunter down Collins Avenue, stop on the way to have a cup of coffee and a sweet roll, enjoy myself, maybe read something out of a newspaper left at the coffee table , go to the dentist and then saunter on back. It was marvelous.

This is our secret palmetto hiding place.
We hid there for hours winning the
camouflage contest.

MIAMI BEACH! WHAT A PLACE FOR BASIC TRAINING!

That's me on the left. I forget the names of the other men. The four of us and little Pete,
developed a very close bond. The goofy silliness that is exhibited here, was typical of us, a
bunch of 18 years olds. The picture at the bottom is of the Normandie Hotel, next door to
ours, the Tides.

FROM MIAMI BEACH TO A...
GERMAN SLAUGHTERHOUSE!

It was late in December 1943. Part of the regimen of being a fledgling air cadet was to guard the shores of Miami Beach.

The sightings of submarines were supposedly made; at least that is what we had heard. It was later proven that German subs came within striking distance of cities on the east coast. There were sinkings of vessels not too far from the shore in those early days of World War II.

A big semi truck dropped a bunch of us off at the outer limits of Miami Beach. My position was isolated so far away from civilization, I felt I was in a different world.

The M1 Garand rifle added very little comfort to my fear. A few months earlier, as an 18 year old kid, I was attending Georgia Tech as a freshman; now here I was in Miami Beach in the middle of winter, alone, on a beach. The winds that came howling in from the depths of darkness made me cold not only externally but internally as well.

My duty was to walk about half a mile south down the beach and turn around and come back the other way, meeting my cohorts as they made their beat in a slow sojourn up and down the windy, dark, damp dreary beaches of Miami.

I was terrified. Fast moving clouds make the shadows of tall, swaying palm trees seemed like people coming towards me. The moonlight was intermittent, the effect of the fast moving clouds creating more frightening shadows. I walked my beat as best I could with as much bravado as I could muster as I met my colleagues north and south of me.

Now fast forward two years later to Germany in an area near the suburbs of Koblenze.

Our squad was directed to guard a largely intact dark red slaughterhouse on the edge of the city. The ramshackle structure seemed to meander around the area much like the path that an escaped steer might make leaving the premises. There were wooden walkways, presumably put there to keep people from walking in the slime generated by the slaughterhouse. The walkway planks were warped and creaked; my boots would stumble over the loose boards—again all painted a dark red.

My orders were to guard the area, to take the path as it wandered around the premises of the structure. We were told there was enemy hiding in parts of this building.

At 2:00 a.m., I was awakened by Al, my foxhole buddy, to begin my two-hour trek. It was the middle of March 1945, I was miserably cold and vestiges of the "aroma" of the slaughtered animals filled my nostrils. Sounds emitting from this environment combined with my discernable oofs and groans as I stumbled in the dark made it more terrifying for me. The sound of flapping shutters in the breeze, creaking doors in the distance – or whatever that was and the footsteps of my cohort – I hope that was him –in the distance, made me shiver.

Thank God nothing happened. After two seemingly never-ending hours, I was relieved by Tony.

These two stories provide nothing of substance as to what it was to be a combat infantry man. They do though provide a flavor of the terror that an eighteen year old feels as he accepts the responsibility to himself and to his colleagues to comport himself properly in every situation. In both cases I was scared almost to the point of terror, yet I believe, had I been confronted by a colleague, my demeanor would show no evidence of that.

FIRE! AT THE TIDES HOTEL...JERGENS LOTION?

I volunteered for the Air Corp when I entered the service and wound up of all places in Miami Beach, Florida!

I will never forget leaving Atlanta, Georgia on a dreary, cold December morning and arriving 14 hours later in gorgeous, verdant, warm Miami Beach!

We were "billeted" in the Tides Hotel. The government took over many of the hotels on Miami Beach and converted them into places where young soldiers stayed during Air Corp basic training. It was a terrific place to be while in the service!

Everything was going along fine until we were assigned a new top Sergeant in charge of our platoon. This guy was born an SOB. He epitomized the DI type, very stern, never smiling, and neat as the perpetually shined "pin." Our nickname for him was Sergeant A.H. He knew it and could not care less.

He got so overbearing that the under-the-breath muttered complaints began to get discernible. Sgt A.H. countered by saying in so many four-letter words, "Tough S—t!"

Billy "Pete" Peterson from Richmond, Virginia had had it. It seemed that Pete was a designated victim for Sgt A.H. practically every week. So, one Saturday night when the Sgt went out on one of his nightly dates while we were confined to our rooms, little Pete got even. He took a condom, put Jergens lotion all in it and around it and hung it on the Sgt's doorknob to his quarters. None of us knew this!

At about 2:00 in the morning one miserable drizzly night in January 1944, the fire alarm goes off. Suddenly we hear Clang! Clang! Clang! Clang! "Damn," we said, "The place is on fire!" We all slept in our underwear. We grabbed our raincoats – you guys remember those things; it was like wearing cold linoleum. We rushed outside to the street. Sgt A.H. was waiting for us.

He barked out, "Line up, and stand at attention."

"What the hell is going on?" we all thought.

The sergeant held up the dripping condom and screamed out, "What son – of – a bitch did this?" We didn't know what he was talking about but it didn't take long before we figured it out. No one looked at little Pete or figured he was the culprit.

Here it was, drizzly, cold, and us in those clammy, cold raincoats in our underwear shaking with cold. The old Sarge kept screaming. No one said a word. No one really knew who did it. After about 40 minutes with much ranting and raving, we were dismissed to go back to our beds literally shivering in our boots.

No one ever admitted to doing it, but we never saw Pete walking around with that hang-dog expression any more. It had changed to a perpetual smiley face.

A BUNCH OF 18 YEAR OLDS GOOFING OFF!!!

A BUNCH OF 18 YEAR OLDS GOOFING OFF!

OUR LOVELY HOME...THE TIDES

WHERE WE WON THE CAMOUFLAGE CONTEST IN THE PALMETTO

POTS AND PANS "KP" AND HOMINY GRITS

It seemed like we were on perpetual KP while in Miami after the condom episode.

Pete was about 5'3" and about 140 pounds. He was the designated pan and pot cleaner. Because I was his best buddy, I was guilty by association and at times, I spelled him in this onerous and odorous job.

One early morning, Pete asked me to help him in doing his breakfast work by doing the pots and pans while he rested a little bit taking the food upstairs to the cafeteria.

Now upstairs was really upstairs. The way the hotel was designed the kitchen was downstairs, accessible by a wide staircase—very wide. I don't know why, that went up to the main floor. We had to carry the food in the mammoth pans of eggs and bacon, etc. up these steps to the dining room.

So, on this fateful day, Ol' Petey hefted a very large heavy tray of hominy grits (for you damn Yankees, hominy grits look like mothballs but are kidney shaped and taste like grit). Man, there were millions of those little balls of grit in that pan.

Petey struggled up the steps. There must have been 30 of them, and he got almost to the top before he noticed out of the corner of his eye what looked like coffee someone had spilled on them. He was wrong. It was grease, not spilled coffee! His foot slipped!

Down goes Petey, but like a good soldier, he tried to maintain the level of that humongous pan! He failed, slipping and falling. In the history of the world, it was the first time that a Niagara Falls of white hominy grits festooned a staircase in the "snow"— "snow" of white oblong hominy grits!

I can still see poor ol' Petey all day long, picking up and throwing away those little kidney shaped globs of grits. He was put on KP for another week for this Grits Caper.

Pete on the left and me, the
Grits Caper and K.P. pros.

SONG BOOK OR THE ARMY AIR CORPS 1943 AND 1944

My personal booklet: "Flight 118," "Training Group 408"

Immediately after getting to Miami Beach to train as an Air Cadet, we were given this little book. It was mimeographed and about 4x5 inches.

On the back of mine I have written in pencil the words to a song that someone must have created themselves. It is hard to decipher.

We were required to sing any time we marched as a group. The word on the back (to what I think was the tune of "Roll out the barrel") are:

Roll out the Army

Roll out the Navy as well

Roll out the Air Force.

We'll bomb the Axis to hell.

Bombs, shells, bayonets

We'll make old Hitler afraid

When we bomb Berlin

Tomorrow in the big air raid.

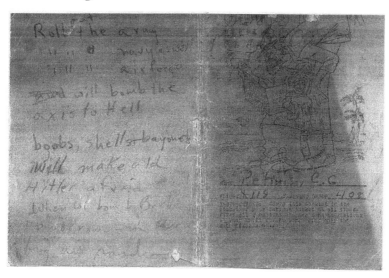

MY SONG BOOK

(23)

(4)

7. REMEMBER PEARL HARBOR

Let's remember Pearl Harbor
As we march against the foe
Let's remember Pearl Harbor
As we did the Alamo
We will always remember
How they died for Liberty
Let's remember Pearl Harbor
And go on to Victory.

8. I'M A YANKEE DOODLE DANDY

I'm a Yankee Doodle Dandy,
A Yankee Doodle do or die
A real live nephew of my Uncle Sam
   born on the 4th of July.
I've got a Yankee Doodle sweetheart
She's my Yankee Doodle joy,
Yankee Doodle came to London just to
   ride the ponies,
I am a Yankee Doodle boy.

9. BRITISH FLYERS' BALLAD

I've got six pence (6-4-2-0)
Jolly, jolly six pence
I've got six pence
To last me all my life
I've got tuppence to spend,
And tuppence to lend,
And tuppence to send home to my wife
No cares have I to grieve me
No pretty little girls to deceive me
I'm happy as a king believe me
As we go rolling, rolling home.
Rolling home! (Rolling home)
Rolling home! (Rolling home)
By the light of the silvery moo-oo-n
Happy is the day
When the airmen gets his pay
As we go rolling, rolling home.

(25)

OTHER FAVORITE SONGS

(2)

4. WORKING ON THE RAILROAD

I've been working on the railroad,
All the live-long day,
I've been working on the railroad,
Just to pass the time away,
Can't you hear the whistle blowing
Rise up so early in the morn,
Can't you hear the Captain shouting,
Dinah, blow your horn.
Dinah, won't you blow,
Dinah, won't you blow,
Dinah won't you blow your ho-o-orn.
Dinah, won't you blow
Dinah, won't you blow.
Dinah won't you blow your horn.
Oh, someone's in the kitchen with Dinah
Someone's in the kitchen I know-o-o-o
Someone's in the kitchen with Dinah,
Strummin' on the old banjo.
Fee, fie, fiddle-dee-aye-oh.
Fee, fie, fiddle-dee-aye-oh-oh-oh-oh
Fee, fie, fiddle-dee-aye-oh
Strummin' on the old banjo.
         G.I. VERSION
I was working in the kitchen
Workin' as a chef
Got a letter from my draft board
And they said, "You ain't 4-F."
So they put me in the Army
Thought I would be a soldier then
I was working in the kitchen
And I'm right back there again.
Private, won't you go, Private, won't you g
Private, won't you go, they nag, nag, nag.
Sergeant won't you blow, Sergeant won't
   you blow, blow it out your barracks bag!
Oh, someone's in the kitchen with Dinah(etc
         2ND VERSE
I was working as a barber
All the livelong day

(5)

10. FAR FAR AWAY

Around her neck she wore a yellow ribbon
She wore it in the springtime and through
    the month of May.
And when you ask the reason why she wore
    it
She says it's for a soldier who is far,
    far away.

CHORUS

Far away (far away) far away (far away)
And she wore it milking cows and mowing
    hay.
For around her neck she wore a yellow
    ribbon
She wore it for a soldier who is far,
    far away

2ND VERSE

Around her neck she wore a little locket
She wore it in the springtime and in the
    month of May.

CHORUS

3RD VERSE

Around her leg she wore a purple garter,
She wore it in the springtime and in the
    month of May.

CHORUS

4TH VERSE

Around her finger she wore a little
    diamond
She wore it in the springtime and in the
    month of May.

CHORUS

5TH VERSE

Around the house she wore a Mother Hubbard
She wore it from September all through
    the month of May.
And when you ask the reason why she wore it

(3)

Then I heard about Pearl Harbor
And enlisted right away.
Thought I'd be a tough commando
Avenging all the Jap attacks
But they gave me special duty
As hairdresser for the WACS.
    (Repeat Chorus)

5. COMING IN ON A WING AND A PRAYER

Coming in on a wing and a prayer
Coming in on a wing and a prayer
Tho' there's one motor gone,
We can still carry on.
Coming in on a wing and a prayer
What a show, what a fight
Yes! we really hit our target for tonight
How we sing as we limp thru the air
Look below there's our field over there
With our full crew aboard and our trust
    in the Lord,
Coming in on a wing and a prayer.

6. PRAISE THE LORD

Praise the Lord and pass the ammunition
Praise the Lord and pass the ammunition
Praise the Lord and pass the ammunition
And we'll all stay free.
Praise the Lord and pass the ammunition
Can't afford to sit around a'wishin'
Praise the Lord, we're all between
    Perdish'on and the deep blue sea!
Yes, the sky pilot said it, you've got to
    give his credit
For a son-of-a-gun of a gunner was he.
----Shouting----Praise the Lord, we're on
    a mighty mission
All aboard, we're not a'goin' fishin'
Praise the Lord and pass the ammunition,
    and we'll all stay free.

(5)

10. FAR FAR AWAY

Around her neck she wore a yellow ribbon
She wore it in the springtime and through
the month of May.
And when you ask the reason why she wore
it
She says it's for a soldier who is far,
far away.

CHORUS

Far away (far away) far away (far away)
And she wore it milking cows and mowing
hay.
For around her neck she wore a yellow
ribbon
She wore it for a soldier who is far,
far away.

2ND VERSE

Around her neck she wore a little locket
She wore it in the springtime and in the
month of May.

CHORUS

3RD VERSE

Around her leg she wore a purple garter,
She wore it in the springtime and in the
month of May.

CHORUS

4TH VERSE

Around her finger she wore a little
diamond
She wore it in the springtime and in the
month of May.

CHORUS

5TH VERSE

Around the house she wore a Mother Hubbard
She wore it from September all through
the month of May.
And when you ask the reason why she wore it

(3)

Then I heard about Pearl Harbor
And enlisted right away.
Thought I'd be a tough commando
Avenging all the Jap attacks
But they gave me special duty
As hairdresser for the WACS.
(Repeat Chorus)

5. COMING IN ON A WING AND A PRAYER

Coming in on a wing and a prayer
Coming in on a wing and a prayer
Tho' there's one motor gone,
We can still carry on.
Coming in on a wing and a prayer
What a show, what a fight
Yes! we really hit our target for tonight
How we sing as we limp thru the air
Look below there's our field over there
With our full crew aboard and our trust
in the Lord,
Coming in on a wing and a prayer.

6. PRAISE THE LORD

Praise the Lord and pass the ammunition
Praise the Lord and pass the ammunition
Praise the Lord and pass the ammunition
And we'll all stay free.
Praise the Lord and pass the ammunition
Can't afford to sit around a'wishin'
Praise the Lord, we're all between
Perdition and the deep blue sea!
Yes, the air pilot said it, you've got to
give him credit,
For a son-of-a-gun of a gunner was he.
----Shortage----Praise the Lord, we're on
a mighty mission
All aboard, we're not a'goin' fishin'
Praise the Lord and pass the ammunition,
and we'll all stay free.

20

THE AMERICAN CAFÉ...EAT FREE WITH "PIFF"

My parents emigrated from Greece in the early 1900's, so World War II was only a few decades in the future. This meant for a great cohesiveness among our clan; a togetherness that was very helpful in every aspect of life for an early immigrant to America.

Not too well known in this country is how philotimos the typical Greek immigrant is. "Philotimo" comes from two Greek words, philos, which means friend, and "timi" which means respect.

Being a spirited young soldier I utilized this friendly trait that the Greek immigrant possessed to my advantage. During my travels for the Army throughout the United States from Florida to California wherever I was stationed, I would manage to get to town to try a local restaurant.

Inevitably I would find establishments with names such as "The New York Café," "Athens Restaurant," "American Café" – typical names of Greek restaurants.

All GIs looked forward to weekend passes. With my Greek heritage backing me up, we'd go into town and start looking for one of these so named eating places. In those days most small cafés had a long white marble top counter with round counter stools. I would direct my cohorts to sit at the counter near the cash register. As we sat and ate, I would concentrate on the permits and signs located on the wall by the register. I'd strain to read the name of the proprietor. I'd look for clues, an American flag together with the blue and white Greek flag, or maybe a large picture showing a seated mustached gentleman holding a fedora on his lap together with a woman standing next to him, neither smiling, most likely the owner's parents.

The kicker would be finding a typical Greek name or one that ends in "os" or "kis." Once I found my quarry, we would sit there, two or three of us, four at the most, at the marble counter, and have a delicious meal. As we lined up to pay at the cash register, I'd say "Is this place by any chance owned by a person from Greece?"

Inevitably the response would be in a typical Greek accent "Yes, serl!"

I'd respond, "Kai ego emay Ellinas! (Well, I am Greek too.)" Then, I'd continue, "Pos eesas te?" which means "How are you doing/How are you?"

Well, that's all that was needed. Immediately we would begin jabbering back and forth in Greek. He would then call toward the kitchen asking those to come out and meet some Greek boys. They would come over and pat us on the back. We never had to pay for a solitary meal!

There was one negative aspect to this "system" though, which I had not considered in my planning. Once the word got out about "Piff's" eating-free-method, I was besieged by my friends—some of whom I had never met—to accompany me on my next sojourn for free eats. Being an entrepreneur (translation "cheap"), I gave some thought to charging them to accompany me. Well, I gave that up after some serious thought. We were on the way to combat, after all.

RATTLESNAKE BOMBER BASE
ARMY AIR BASE PYOTE, TEXAS

The only thing consistent with being in the service was the inconsistency of the actions taken by those in charge.

We left Miami bound for somewhere; no one knew our destination, or so we were told. We traveled in regular, but old cars with one major difference, no dining car. Well, we did have one, sort of. It was a boxcar outfitted quite differently, equipped very much like the mobile kitchens that were used overseas in combat. Large metal barrels served many uses from cooking to storing things, to hot water for rinsing one's utensils and mess kit. The "kitchen car" was at the end of a very long string of cars.

I guess the stoves burned wood or charcoal, I don't know. I do know that the smoke was unbearable for the poor GIs on kitchen duty and for us as we threaded our way to the food lines and then U-turned back.

We traveled for days! From Miami, we went to Austin, Texas, then up to Salt Lake City, then to Colton, California. Finally, eastwardly again, it slowed near El Paso, and then did the same at Monahans, Texas, finally stopping—for me, at Pyote, Texas.

The terrain was flat. I mean F.L.A.T. ! As we got off of the bus, we were directed to supply, where we were issued new solid leather boots and a .45 pistol "for killing the rattlers."

"Damn! Rattlers? Miami, where are you?" went through my mind.

Another unique geographic aspect of the terrain was the multitude and size of the tumbleweeds. That is a misnomer—they were TUMBLE "WOODS," gigantic things that roamed at will and went out of their way to run you over. The wind! The WIND was in concert with them. It blew constantly at 20 to 40 miles per hour….all the time. All of the barracks were held down by 4 quarter inch cables, to keep them anchored so they would not go the way of the tumbleweeds. The cables were an environmental hazard to those of us that got home drunk. Banged heads, ankles, knees, shins were all candidates for that era of cable "news." So now you get the picture. And now…I will show you some!

RATTLESNAKE BOMBER BASE ARIEL VIEW

ME WISHING I WAS PILOTING A B17 BOMBER

THAT'S ME

B29'S.. THAT DROPPED THE ATOM BOMBS.
PYOTE WAS THE FIRST BASE TO ACCOMODATE THE
B29 SUPER FLYING FORTRESS

B17'S

MY OWN JEEP!

THOSE DAMN TUMBLE WEEDS!

GUN CAMERA BUILDINGS

QUIT DOING THAT PEETEY! IT TICKLES!

It was hot as blazes in Pyote, Texas. Except for our rigged up air conditioned photo lab office, all we had to cool our barracks was a large fan, so this forced us to sleep in our skivvies.

In my group was David who was a womanizer and would regale us with his fictionalized stories of his conquests of women. That is the closest thing we had to porn in 1944.

One of the known "facts" about young men of that age group is that when a male is sleeping, you could put his hand in a container of warm water. This action supposedly would trigger a physiological response which would make him pee his pants — or in our case, skivvies.

We tried this on David several times, who seemed like he was always taking a nap. It never worked.

"Peetey" Peterson, the name, came from his pissing on the barracks that housed our officers in Pyote, would get drunk out of his mind in downtown in Monahans, Texas. We would sort of "pour" him on a bus after one of his weekly beer binges. Being too big and heavy to carry, we would help him stagger to his barracks. Along the way, he would insist that we weave him towards the BOQs (Bachelor Officer's Quarters) so that he could pee upon the building. Artistic in temperament, he tried to "write" "Pete" on the wall as an artist does when signing a work of art.

Peetey was not much of a ladies' man. He was always envious of David's female conquests though he very much doubted their authenticity.

One very hot August Saturday afternoon, Peety gets a bright idea to test David's manliness and testosterone level. David had an incredible solution in fighting those hot Texas afternoons: he would sleep through them. This made the rest of us mad as hell; none of us were blessed with this genetic aberration.

Now Peetey, had received a gift from home in Arkansas, strange as it sounds, a brush made of beautiful turkey feathers. His father, an ardent turkey hunter, had made the brush "by his OWN hands!" Peetey would proudly use it to brush the dust from around the area of his bunk.

On this particular Saturday afternoon, Peety goes up to the slumbering, supine David and begins to very carefully expose David's penis from the constraints of his boxer shorts (the rest of us wore the jockey type).

We all watched mesmerized barely breathing at this fiendish scheme. We had no idea what he was up to. Remarkably he succeeded perfectly. Poor David's penis lay exposed to the world and to the heat.

Peetey then took a feather from his trophy dusting brush, a very long one, and began gently and carefully to stroke David's sleeping penis — up and down, up and down, he continued. Magically David's penis began to feel the effect. We stood there, our eyes glued to this phenomenon being created right before our eyes. Slowly David's penis began rising, accompanied by a slow moaning sound from David's partially opened lips.

Peetey continued the stroking faster and faster, and David's moans became louder and louder. He began thrashing around the bed still on his back. By then, we, the audience, decided to leave. Visions of what David would do to Peetey's face made that an appropriate decision.

By now David had a handsome erection. At that instant, luckily for Peetey, in walks our barracks Sergeant. The Sergeant had not seen the stroking. All that he saw was a soldier indecently exposing his genitals. Old Sarge, screaming at David, says "Wake up, you son of a bitch! What the hell do you think you are doing?"

Poor David woke up wild eyed, yelling, "What happened? What happened?" Poor Mr. Penis retracted himself –turtle like.

Ol' Sarge responded in words too undecipherable and too vivid for this story.

After that, poor David's sleeping in hot afternoons subsided, much like the effect on Mr. Penis.

SWIMMING AT BIG SPRINGS, TEXAS.

THAT'S ME ON THE RIGHT OF THE THREE. DAVID IS ONE OF THE OTHER TWO.

PEETY IS ON THE RIGHT....SOBER!

WHAT STINKS?!? I THINK IT'S YOUR TOBACCO!!

One of the realities of being in the armed services is that one cannot select one's colleagues or roommates. One of the lower rank sergeants in our group at Peyote, Texas was David Smith (we'll call him that). His name was not Smith—it was an Irish name. Our poor David, a very nice gentleman, would never take a bath. In fact, you could sense (or smell) his presence when he walked into the barracks.

He was an avid and professional pipe smoker. He had several Meerschaum pipes, all of which he handled very carefully. He also insisted upon importing his tobacco house in Chicago.

As to the shower situation, we finally threatened David that if he did not take a bath at least three times a week, we would literally give him a G.I. bath once a week. This meant scrubbing him with G.I. brushes, in softness, not unlike Brillo pads.

Well, we finally did it. After we got through with his first and –fortunately for us—last (what is more repulsive than scrubbing down a fellow male person? Nothing!) G.I. bath, Ol' David became Mr. Clean thereafter.

Now, as to the especially ordered, blended tobacco from Chicago, here is what I did.

I swept the floor accumulating a supply of dirt, detritus, and hairs. To this odiferous mixture, I added the shavings from our pencil sharpener. The rubber was obtained by "sharpening" the eraser.

Now our David, a sweet but innocent fellow, decided one day to light up his favorite Meerschaum pipe, a beauty with a white bowl and a shiny wood and plastic stem. It was a gorgeous instrument! We all waited expectantly while he carefully packed the "our tobacco" into the bowl. He lit it, and began smoking contentedly. No reaction, none at all! We all watched. Tony next to me whispered, "Hey, Piff, didja notice how the eraser stuff sort of bubbles and sputters as it burns?"

"Yep," I responded, still mesmerized by David's being oblivious to the uniqueness of his "special blend from Chicago" and now from Pyote Texas!

David beat us, I'm sorry to say. He smoked the whole damn can of the stuff, inundated with the detritus of our quarters and some pencil stuff! He never complained or commented, he just smoked!

Tony, me, and David in the photo lab. The other picture is the Gun Camera crew celebrating the news from a telegram, announcing the birth of Sam's first child.

OH NO! I DIDN'T!....OH YES YOU DID!

Before being transferred to the infantry, I had a dream job at Peyote, Texas at the—would you believe—Rattlesnake Army Airbase. My job was as a technician in the developing of motion pictures taken by cameras of training dogfights between P47 fighters and B-17 bombers. It was an amazing activity.

We installed the cameras in the gun placements of the P47s. The pilots would get into a dogfight with the B-17s and instead of firing bullets; they would "fire" pictures of the action.

Our job once the actions ceased was to take the cameras from the planes, carefully remove the film, and process it in very large automated processing machines.

On one beautiful April day in 1944, a fledgling group of young pilots came to Peyote to get this important training. We had heard that within this group there was a young hotshot pilot that everyone revered but frankly was somewhat afraid of because of his daring and skill.

Our complete crew would go out to the tarmac to watch the '47s take off and have to combat the B-17s. We could see the dogfight but not too clearly because the planes were so high.

One of the B-17s for some reason was delayed and managed to lumber off a few moments after the others. As it rose into the sky, we were stunned to see a '47 peel off and head right for the 17 even though they were both only a few thousand feet high. Suddenly, there was a sharp crack of noise. Bits of debris started falling toward the ground. The '47s right wing had clipped the tail of the 17. Except for a sudden veering of the two crafts, the pilots maintained control of both planes, circled and landed.

All hell broke loose! Fire engines, their sirens bellowing, circled the planes but luckily they were not needed. The pilots, we learned later, each blamed the other for the mishap. The P47 pilot was the young hotshot.

I rushed to the P47 and quickly removed its gun cameras. I went to the photo lab to remove the film for processing. Our officer in charge stopped me, saying he would do the processing himself. Apparently this job was too important for some novice like me to do the processing. After all, these films would show exactly what happened and which pilot was at fault.

Feeling somewhat chastised, we left the lieutenant and went to the chow hall for lunch. It would take about an hour or so to do the processing so after lunch we went immediately to the photo lab to see what was happening. As we walked in, we saw the lieutenant sitting, white as a ghost, sitting in his office chair, feet on the desk, fanning himself with the perspiration running down his face.

Our esteemed leader, not doing this job too often, but leaving it to us peons, had unfortunately pressed the wrong button, thereby blackening the film, not having one image come out whatsoever.

I will never forget the look on his face as the commander of the base, a colonel, walked in asking for the film which was to be flown somewhere where some generals wanted to see it. Poor guy—he was a good guy. Never heard from him again—he was probably transferred to the infantry like I was.

The small picture is our commanding officer Lt. Leverault.
Poor guy hit the wrong button. Also that's me and Collins,
worn out at about 3am.

These are from inside the Gun Camera Section. We had to
show the actual film that was shot during the make believe
dog fight.

That's me on the left at the movie machine. The three men
are: Caruso, me and David (the smoker of imported tobacco
to which I added my special blend of detritus swept up from
the floor with added pencil eraser shavings for flavor.

Me again at the board and next, Sanders and Goodman at a
large image machine.

COOLED BEER BOTTLES & A GIGANTIC FIST!

When I was drafted in the Army in November 1943, I requested that I go into pilot training. As a youngster I spent a lot of my time reading about the World War I Aces, both American and German, like Germany's Red Baron and Eddie Rickenbacker of the US.

I saw no reason that I could not qualify. I was in perfect health, having passed the most stringent physical examinations. Finally, I was on my way to becoming a hot shot pilot, my dream!

There were several tests given us, the last of which was a psychomotor test. This is very hard to explain but as I began, I felt as if I was operating in slow motion. The test gauged one's dexterity in coordinating physically the eyes and hands, much like using a lathe in a machine shop.

As I began, I knew I would fail this test. It is so strange, even after all of these years, I can sense how it felt. So I flunked, to the dismay of my friends, all of whom would be going to flight schools, probably in Texas somewhere.

I was the one that went to Texas, and the other men were sent to locations throughout the United States. I was assigned as a film laboratory technician at an Army Air Corps base at Peyote, Texas, known as "Rattlesnake Army Air Base" (the place was overrun by rattlers. We wore heavy boots and carried a side arm!) not too far from Big Springs and El Paso.

There are several things that stand out in my mind about that session in those months at Peyote. First, somehow I had gotten myself a Jeep, which was wonderful! Secondly, the cafeteria was opened twenty-four hours a day (I loved to have a snack at midnight) to service the air crews as they came from after-hours training. Third, because our function was to process the film from the gun cameras which were used in lieu of machine guns as P 47 pilots shot at B-17s and B-26s, we were looked upon almost in awe.

Next, we probably had the only air conditioned facility in Texas—probably in all the country. Antoine—that was his name—hard to believe because besides being a womanizer he could repair or create anything, rigged up a window sized box with double frames. The sides were made of wire, the kind used at farms to contain chickens.

He then stuffed all four sides with straw. This configuration was then connected to a hose pipe. The portion of the pipe that ran parallel to the top of the window had holes in it. This allowed water to drip slowly down and through the straw. A large fan was placed at the window to pull the outside air in. This worked because the outside air was so dry. Man, that was one cool contraption—in more ways than one!

Antoine, who loved his beer, also came up with a scheme to keep his favorite libation stored where it was always cool. Ingeniously he noted that the containers that the unexposed film came in were sitting stored empty in the closet. Each container would magically hold two bottles of beer.

Suddenly, it seemed we had several rolls of unexposed film that had to be kept cool and unexposed. One day we had a snap inspection by a captain from a different area. He questioned the need of a refrigerator in a lab such as ours. He opened the door, looked inside to an array of containers very carefully noted on adhesive tape "Unexposed film—DO NOT OPEN!:

Another one of our colleagues in my group was about 40 years old and rather rotund and soft. He was a nice guy but sort of creepy. When I arrived there as a new replacement, he could not have been more solicitous.   The other men were not, but this guy was.

I had requested a furlough to Atlanta for Christmas holidays. I was surprised to hear that my rotund friend was also heading east. We'd be on the same train. For some reason—which I've totally forgotten—we had to change trains in east Texas, requiring us to spend the night in sort of a motel. In those days, there was no air conditioning. To alleviate that, each room, where the walls met the ceiling, had slats of wood there in lieu of solid wall. This allowed air to flow and circulate from room to room. The slatted height was about 30 inches (you could smell cigarette smoke if someone was smoking next door).

There were two single beds in our room. Mine was near the wall; his was more or less in the center. About two o'clock in the morning, I woke to the sound of a scraping sound. My friend had moved his bed next to mine. When I asked why, he said to allow more breeze to hit him because "it would bounce off the wall," etc. Dummy me, all of 18 years old, I understood.

About four in the morning, I awakened to the feeling of "Rotund's" massive leg across my legs. He woke up with a start as I pushed his leg off of me. He sort of snorted and apologized saying he was having a bad dream and turned over and went to sleep. Yean, I thought, like hell he's sleeping.

Man, I was pissed! I thought to myself, "You fat son-of-a- bitch. I ought to kick your fat ass!" So, I too, pretended to fall back asleep. Now, you will not believe the next statement, but it absolutely happened!

After a few minutes, he snorted and turned over where he faced me. We were now "looking" at each other but "sleeping." He began his next movement sort of towards me. I lifted my right arm straight up, my hand in a tight fist. At that exact moment, the person in the room to our left got up and turned his light on. His light came through the slats in the ceiling. The angle of the light hit my upraised arm and fist. The shadow was awesome! I possessed a gigantic fist!

Ol' brother "Rotund" snorted and turned over, now facing the other direction. I got up, turned the light on, and pushed his bed all the way against the opposite wall. No words were spoken. He got the message loud and clear!

HITCH HIKING HOME ON A
B-17 FLYING FORTRESS BOMBER

One of the great perks on being a ground crew member at an air base was the ability to hitch hike home on an airplane. I did it several times.

Because I was assigned to the Gun Camera section, I got to know many of the pilots pretty well. After we would remove the film from the gun cameras and processed it, I would show the film on a 16 mm projector to all the pilots, both for the B-17's and P-47's.

One day in 1944, I looked at the Board in the flight room where pilots posted their training flights. Listed was a flight leaving in just a few minutes with a pilot that I had gotten to know. He too was from Atlanta. I had gotten permission for a three day pass. The flight was heading to Montgomery, Alabama. Not too bad, about 170 miles from my home town.

I rushed back to the barracks and got my stuff almost all packed. I sprinted across the tarmac, just as the pilot was about to rev up the motors. One of my buddies, (Mac) "Mackey" so called because he was so small and thin – we wondered if the recruitment guy made a mistake to allow him to be drafted – saw me coming and yelled to hurry up. I made it no sweat.

There were 12 guys on the plane mostly crew and we hitchhikers. As we entered the air space over Alabama, the right most engine began smoking. "Oh shit" murmured through the craft. The pilot feathered it and we kept going, no problem. (These magnificent planes could fly quite well on only two engines.)

About 5 minutes late, the engine at the extreme left began smoking and sort of vibrating. It got feathered too. Over the speaker came the pilot's voice very calm, "Guys better hook on your parachutes." Now we all were wearing the vest like harness to which one would click on the actual chute. There was a hurried grab at the pile of chutes that were lying around the guys. We all put them on but me. I was number 13 for only 12 chutes!

There was not really too much sympathy expressed by my colleagues just stoic faces . . . . translated, "Tough shit" . . . . <u>late</u> arriver!

Well little did my good friend Mackey realize that if he jumped out with his chute he would not be alone. 'Cause ol' Charlie boy was going to piggy back upon him all the way down, face to face almost kissin' my little friend!

No sweat, no chutes, no kissin', we landed fine in good ol' Montgomery. (I'd been there many times before.) Now I had to hitch hike by car to Atlanta. Luckily one of the guys lived there so his folks gave me a ride to the main highway to Atlanta. I stood there for about 15 minutes with my thumb stuck out wearing an earnest please-give-this-soldier-who-is-going-home-smile-a-ride.

Well I got a ride all right. Of all things in a "luxurious" black, muddy, beat up, rattley   1938 Ford pick up truck. The driver was an aging gent about 70 with a toothy, gapped grin. "Git in solja - real Surthern- he said. Where you goin' Atlana? "Yes sir", I answered and clambered in the back. "Seated" next to him was a bunch of greasy tractor parts.

Luckily the weather was warm so you could think I was riding in sort of a convertible with the top down. However I was not the only passenger in this "convertible". There were about 20 others . . . . . .squawking chickens in two wooden crates and more black greasy tractor parts spread everywhere.

We got to Atlanta o.k. I got a ride in another truck all the way out to Druid Hills. The guy, who had a son in the service, took me to the very door of our home.

Well I rang the door bell. Mom opened it and screamed at the surprise – I had not told them fearing that maybe I would not make it. She jumped to hug me but stopped short. Who'd want to hug a wind blown soldier whose uniform was streaked with black tractor grease and a few hanging feathers that I had missed still hanging from my clothes.

Dad being a traveling salesman rearranged his selling schedule to go to Montgomery. We left early Monday morning. I met up with my friends and flew back to the Rattlesnake Bomber Air base in Peyote, Texas.

I did not realize that upon my leaving for Atlanta, my adventure would include "feathering" two engines and myself too!

YIKES! WOW! I'VE GOT A RED HOT BOTTOM!!

In early January 1945, I started infantry basic training at Camp Howzey (near Paris) Texas. We called it Camp Lowzey.

In our new group of aspiring infantrymen was Mike. Mike was from the Deep South somewhere and was a finagler par excellence! Mike's family was in the plumbing business covering everything from cesspools to installing plumbing in fancy hotels.

For some reason which we could not comprehend, camp "Lowzey" had the hottest water in the world!

Fresh, downy faced, young recruits were arriving each day. Mike suddenly had a brainstorm! Working feverishly one night with several of us holding flashlights, Mike somehow managed to divert the plumbing to one of the toilets from cold water to the steaming hot variety. Somehow too, he managed to make the pressure two or three times greater.

As a new recruit came in to sit on one of the toilets—all of which were exposed (as we all know), somehow a whole bunch of guys suddenly had "to go." Only one toilet was unoccupied. Guess which one! We waited expectantly for the victim to flush.

Oh, man! There was much hooting, hollering, and screaming; the screaming coming from the "red bottom" victim.

They looked at us culprits with utter disdain and revulsion, but I noticed as time progressed that these "red bottom" persons were the first to designate a new, downy-faced recruit to be the next "red bottom" victim!

MISSION IN THE WILDS OF PARIS, TEXAS

We had a Gung-Ho and a pain in the you-know-what captain at Camp Howzey, Texas, but we had a great lieutenant!

One night we were out on a "mission" to conquer the "enemy" in the Texas woods, in other words, playing grown-up cowboys and Indians about 20 miles out in the Texas "wilderness."

It was cold, raining, foggy, miserable, miserable weather in the middle of December. We marched—trudged—back 10 miles, dog-tired, soaking wet, freezing. Our boots were sopping wet. The tents were still up but the ground below them was wet. We were a miserable hell of a mess.

We had just settled down for the night trying to keep warm, taking our boots off and trying to dry them by barn fires. All of a sudden, the lieutenant comes by, sticks his head in each tent and says, "Sorry guys, the captain wants another session like we just finished. We have to repeat what we did before."

Talk about being pissed! You never heard so many moans, groans and curses and all kinds of expletives using the captains name in there somewhere.

So we formed out near the big bonfire still moaning and bitching, trying to put our wet boots over wet socks—damn near impossible! Talk about miserable and steaming! Unbelievable!

The lieutenant then utters some words, almost whispering, and we couldn't believe what he said! "Okay, guys, gather around. We are going to march out of here away from the fire, away out into the darkness. You will line up in formation. Then you begin, and I will hear, 'hut, two, three, four, hut, two, three, four' as we have always done, but as you get further away from the light you say those words much softer as if we are yards away. Proceed doing that as you are getting further away from where we are camped, where the final 'hut, two, three, four' can barely be heard. Then you guys sneak back, get in your tents and keep damn quiet. Don't anybody move or say one word. We are not even here! Now, three o'clock sharp, you sneak out of your tents, go into the woods away from the light, and reverse the process. Come marching back to the area as if we have been out there for three hours. Your 'hut, two, three, four; will be soft at first, getting louder as you get "nearer" the camp. Get it?!" Man, we got it!

We could not believe our ears. We would have died for this guy on the spot. We did exactly what he said to do. It worked perfectly. Unless the ol' captain is alive and reading this book, no one ever knew about it but us!

I SCRAPED BY...ALMOST NAKED!

Prior to being transferred to the infantry I was in the Air Corps stationed at Peyote, Texas at the Rattlesnake Army Air Base. It was a dream job. Our small group processed the film generated by fighter pilots "shooting" 16mm film of B-17s and B-24s when they practiced air combat with P47s. We all wore coveralls. Being a "cool guy," I had mine tailored so they fit well around my waist. I did not like all the flopping around that comes with coveralls! I bleached them so much that they were very light green, not the old ugly Army green!

All of a sudden I am transferred to the infantry to Camp Howzey, near Paris, Texas. We went through all the regular basic training the infantry guys go through in an abbreviated form, one of which was crawling with your rifle—as we have all done—under barbed wire with explosives going off around you while machine-guns shot live ammunition with the tracers over our heads. To make matters worse, the ground was hard and full of pebbles. To make it messy for us, it was wetted down so we were crawling through mud and pebbles with bullets flying over!

I did my duty, crawling perfectly and got up triumphantly with nary a scratch. My coveralls of course were caked in mud and pebbles. So, being "innovative and brilliant" I got out my trusty bayonet and began scraping the mud and the pebbles off my chest down to my crotch, and down to my thighs. To my dismay and alarm I saw I was scraping my coveralls off! I had bleached them so much to make them nice, soft and sexy, that the weakened fabric literally came off with the mud.

Here I am standing there with all the guys guffawing with laughter, with one-half of my underwear showing—the front half! The two sleeves were attached at the back. The "trousers" were attached at the rear end and my chest was exposed.

The captain, hearing the ruckus, came running over. He remarked with all kinds of expletives, "What the hell is wrong with you, Pefinis?"

"Sir," I explained, "Apparently my uniform fabric was very weak and it just came off."

"Damn," he said, "I can't have you looking like that marching through these small towns. Go back with me in my jeep. You won't scare any civilians if they can't see that mess! We'll be a mockery for the whole Army. Also, take some rope and tie all the parts of those coveralls together so at least they'll stay on!"

"Yes Sir!" I said. Then, to myself, "Hell, I'm going to ride back while these poor guys are going to have to march 20 miles back."

I actually did "tie one on." I tied a lot on. Rope tied together each sleeve and the trousers. Man, I was a ropey, mud flecked mess! But, I was elated — apparently elated too much, I guess. When the captain saw my expression, he changed his mind and said, "Oh, no, I am not going to do that Pefinis, you look too happy." He then turned to the Sergeant and said, "Make sure when this guy goes through these towns you put a bunch of guys around him so he won't embarrass us." Damn, I thought, I thought I had managed to "scrape" by, not having to march those 20 miles!

By the time we got back to the camp, the kitchen had closed. We were ravenous — starving! But, no food — except the food I hated — stewed tomatoes, was available. Man we--I — chowed down on those delicious can't-get-enough-of-them-stewed-tomatoes!

MUSCLE BOUND AND CMH BOUND...YEAH!

We left New York on the USS America, now converted to an Army transport. It was a glorious ship. All the grandeur, the furnishings, the decorations were still intact, designated by the US government to carry troops to Europe.

We were jammed, literally jammed at each level, guys almost on top of each other. I developed a friendship with a couple of my newfound friends. The discussion ranged from being terrified to one of these days I will get myself a CMH—Congressional Medal of Honor—Yeah, that's a bunch of 18-year-old malarkey.

One of our erstwhile friends Tony, a handsome young Italian gentleman, was from New Jersey. He was a superb and well endowed weight lifter. He had muscles in places I never knew existed. He was very proud of his muscular look and strength—really a very nice guy.

Since we all assumed that we were going into battle, the thought was that "Tony who is bright, tough, strong as hell, would be a great guy to be with when things start happening."

About the third day out of New York, there was a heavy storm, gale-like winds and heavy seas. It was cold as blazes, and suddenly we heard over the speaker, "Now hear this. "There is a submarine in the area, don your life jackets." This was repeated time and time again, accompanied by clanging bells. Man, did we move.

Now Tony's bunk was two decks down from ours. That's also where his life jacket was. We quickly put ours on and in a moment Tony was back wearing his life jacket. We were amazed how fast Tony was. If there was any doubt as to the reality of being next to Tony in battle, it was certainly erased at that moment.

We all rushed up to the upper deck getting ready to board the life boats if necessary. Luckily it was a false alarm. Three days later we were in Glasgow, Scotland, finally arriving in Europe, where our great adventure would begin.

It took a while for us to get from Glasgow to England, from England across the channel to France at La Havre, so then we were in Belgium. We all separated going to different units. Tony went to a company in our regiment but not in my battalion. One of his close buddies that he developed on the ship, who is in our battalion, visited Tony now and then.

One day, he came back ashen faced. "Guess what, guys, Tony's been shot!"

"Really," I said, "How did it happen?"

"Would you believe the son of a bitch shot himself in the arm?"

"You've got to be kidding!"

"No, that's the truth. The guy is an idiot. He shot himself, so not to bleed to death, then wrapped the towel around his arm, which is okay, I guess, but would you believe the dumb bastard had the towel wrapped around his arm and then pulled the trigger! Smart! Holes in his arm and holes in a towel."

So, that's the story of our future, muscle-bound Congressional Medal of Honor winner. I think poor ol' Tony had a muscle-bound brain. It takes all kinds!

MOP DETAIL ON THE USS AMERICA

Thoughts of my going over and coming back on the USS America:

While going over, I had the distinct pleasure with four of my colleagues to be on the mop detail in the kitchen—better described as a behemoth kitchen! It was as long as a football field.

It was late January, 1945 and the weather was pretty bad in the Atlantic. Even though we were on a gigantic vessel, it was tossed around like an eggshell.

Whoever designed that ship was pretty smart. In the kitchen floor and the walls were all tile with the tile curving up from the floor to make a wall. That made for no cracks to clean between the wall and the floor. It also made a nice toboggan type ride as we "rode" our mops while "mopping."

Our job was to wipe the floors when anything was spilled. We did this diligently. For some reason, none of my crew was seasick—most guys were—even though we were around all this food slopping and spilled on the floor.

One night it got so bad that one of the guys got the bright idea of "riding" his mop by standing on it. As the ship lurched sideways and up and down, we would "ride" the mops on the floor against the wall and, believe it or not, up the wall a few inches!

There we were, a bunch of "warriors" – fresh 18-year-old kids—going off to war learning how to do it by "riding" our mops!

One day we had sausages for lunch. Man, the sea was so rough nobody was eating except us, the mop detail. Everybody was throwing up—except we "moppers!"

I will never forget the sight of seeing that gigantic stainless steel cooking pot being manhandled over the side of the ship and the cascade—a Niagara Fall of red sausage going into the sea! The fish really had a feast that day. None of the guys were eating!

A FAT AND TOASTY WARM, FOXHOLE FRIEND

There were all types in our group. Carlos Valdez—not his real name—was a pimp in New York in civilian life. We had the watchmaker, we had the farmer, we had the carpenter, we had the auto salesman and the pimp ("Piff, when theez is over, come to New York. I'll feex you up with as many guls as you want for free! Won't cost you a dime.")

As a replacement, I arrived in Germany the latter part of February 1945 during a driving snowstorm and was assigned a spot at the top of a knoll and began trying to dig a foxhole in frozen soil. I was to become an ammo carrier for a machine gun unit. Our sergeant told us to select another replacement and work at this foxhole situation together.

Being 19 years old and frightened, with eyes opened in wonderment, but still having a finagler's brain, I picked old Jim Pappernick—not his real name. Jim was a fine young man about 40 pounds overweight and so flatfooted that we joked that he would wear out the insteps of his shoes before the heels or toes. We never knew how the man got drafted in the first place and particularly being put in the infantry. Pappernick was my buddy. We dug the hole though very difficult. The ground was like a rock. My hands were freezing. It snowed all night, the temperature in the low teens. We covered our hole with our raincoats which had the consistency and flexibility of a piece of light linoleum—at least they were waterproof.

We woke up to see the landscape dotted by little mounds of snow on the flat terrain. The mounds were the two sleeping guys covered by their raincoats. I believe ours was the only one that stood out as dark green rather than snow white. Old buddy Pappernick, so nice and warm and fat, he was toasty warm. His and my body generated enough warmth to melt the snow. Granted, it made our foxhole sort of muddy and exposed, but who cared about that. I had made the right selection. I was not too much later when old Pappernick was transferred to the supply area because of his flat feet.

Now one of our buddies, from Wisconsin was Kuntz. That's what his name was. We giggled but he took it in stride. Kuntz came from a German family; his parents immigrated a few years before he was born. The whole clan spoke perfect German as did Kuntz.

This was not too bad, in fact it was great to have such a perfect interpreter in our squad, but unfortunately Kuntz had a bad problem. He had nightmares.

Now think about this, you are dug in for the night, you are terrified, it is pitch black, you do your two hours on, two hours off duty, standing by the perimeter, all your buddies are either on guard with you or sleeping spread around a few hundred yards. Everything is quiet. You listen for any sound that may indicate a person coming through the woods for you — obviously the enemy. We were young, we were bright, we were terrified, and we wanted to live.

The first night it happened, it scared the hell out of us. All of a sudden right in the midst of our foxholes behind the main line, a German voice began speaking in German saying all kinds of weird things. We were stunned. Had we been infiltrated by a German? Was he right in our area screaming at us? As we quickly grabbed our weapons, the calm voice of our platoon sergeant says, "Okay guys, settle down, there ain't no Germans here, it's that damn kid Kuntz screamin in his sleep again."

Kuntz would have these nightmares and speak out so loud in perfect German. Luckily his foxhole buddies had heard this before and knew all about this phenomenon.

Finally with a desperate request to our company commander Kuntz was sent back to somewhere where he could not wake up screaming and scaring the hell out of us.

88 SHELLS....PILLOWS...AND....CHEESE?

My first night in combat took place in Belgium. I was volunteered as an ammunition carrier with a .30mm machine gun crew. We dug in on top of a hill. Mesmerized, we witnessed a barrage of our guns and Jerry's with shells screaming an arc over our heads—terrifying! It was cold, snowing and miserable.

I had dug my foxhole with a new friend, Papernick from New Jersey, also a replacement. To our left, at a higher elevation dug in a deep hole, were two veteran solders of Company B. The 88's, the most feared German artillery piece, were raining down shells on us. One shell hit at the mouth of their hole and poked it steaming nose right in their faces. It did not explode.

The 88 shell must have been invented by the designer of the Stuker with its unnerving scream as it dove. The 88 shell had this high, shrill scream as it descended. It was terrifying. This brings to mind what many vets experienced at Georgia Tech. In 1946 when I started, the vast majority of the students were veterans. I remember on several occasions when an Air Force jet would fly over at a low altitude, the noise created was such that some guys would hit the ground – a la an 88 shell incoming.

Magically the next night we were ensconced in a beautiful small home, two stories, well kept, perfectly clean, well stocked with food. My new buddy Al and I marked one of the bedrooms on the second floor, as our spot to sleep on—unbelievably—a luxurious, soft, wonderful bed! But these beds were different. I do not know why the German people favored these very, very large down-filled pillows. They were about half the size of the mattress. Nevertheless, it was luxurious comfort.

I always carried a small German dictionary with me though I rarely used it. It would come in handy tonight I thought. For in this neat little home were large loafs of pumpernickel-like bread stored in the rafters. Weird but that is a fact.

You could see them about 8 feet high balanced/cradled carefully on 2x4 boards. We'd knock them down at times but they were very tough to eat, very hard to chew and strong tasting.

We were starving; K rations had no appeal that night. So I took my little dictionary, went into one of the rooms and started asking the home owners to bring me a large head of cheese—one of the guys swore that he had seen one there earlier.

They looked at me like I was insane. They kept lookin down at my shoes and then theirs with a bewildered look on their faces. Frustrated, I left and went to find Kuntz, our "translator" (he was from Wisconsin, a first generation German American who dreamed out loud in his sleep, speaking German!).

"Hey Kuntz," I said, "what am I saying wrong?" I then told him what I had asked.

In a burst of laughter, he replied, "You dumb ass. You were asking them for a large shoe not cheese!"

Ol' Kuntz babbled something to them. They all started laughing, but brought forth the cheese. We all joined together, Germans and GIs eating hard-as-hell-to-chew bread and some great cheese.

GOD IN COMBAT...A GRANDMOTHER'S LOVE

"Whatcha got there, Piff?" Dutch asked as I tried to open a small cardboard box that had just arrived from my mother in Atlanta. "Damn, Piff, the way that thing is wrapped there must be gold in there or something," he continued. He was right; layer after layer of paper and scotch tape had to be unraveled to get to the inside.

"My darling son," the letter began, *"We read in the paper about all the action that the Third Army has seen and we are very worried about you."* I thought back for a moment how terrified my family was when I told them that I was transferred from a cushy job in the Air Corp to a front line infantryman in the 87th Infantry Division—one of General Patton's. My mother and two sisters cried. My father, though, was proud and with eyes that were moist, he hugged me tightly.

"We pray for you each day," the letter continued, *"and have Father offer prayers for you at each church service. Take the cotton out very carefully, and you will see a small 'feelakto'* (a Greek religious medal). *YiaYia* (Granny) *sent it to you to protect you and to bring you back to us. It has been in the family for generations and it has saved many lives. Inside is a tiny splinter from Jesus' cross. You must tape it somewhere on your body, not an arm or a leg, but on your side or chest. Wear it with God's love and ours, and wear it when you return. We love you and pray for you. –Mother."*

As I unwrapped the cellophane, Dutch read the letter and said, "Wow, let's see that thing!" It was thin a little larger than a dime, gold, with a figure of Jesus on one side. On the other side are two figures. One is of St. Constantine and the other that of his mother Elene (Helen). St. Elene, after much effort, located the cross.

I grasped it tightly in my hand and walked over to Joe Kanowski, our medic, and got adhesive tape from him. Dutch helped me carefully tape it over my heart.

"Man, Piff," Dutch said, "Buddy, I am stickin close with you, maybe some of that protection will rub off on me." From that moment on I felt different, a feeling of peace, yet one of strength too.

"Dutch," I said, "This thing really makes me feel different."

"Oh hell, Piff, you are just imagining things," he said. But I really felt quite different.

There were four battle situations that followed after that that I knew of the protection this little amulet afforded me.

The first happened a few days later, while running across an open road and field a machine gun opened up. Bullets that come close to one's head make a snapping noise like when you snap your fingers. The snaps were all around my head.

A 80 mm shell plummeted down towards me and two friends. It hit at our feet and did not explode.

While in a house looking for Krauts, a mortar shell shattered a window, hit and bounced all over the room, and did not explode.

Panzer tanks opened on four of us at point blank range at a road block. I did not get a scratch. Two men died.

There is no question in my mind that my Grandmother's (a VERY religious woman) and my family's prayers plus a splinter from the cross upon which Jesus was crucified, saved my life.

THE GOLD AMULET. IT CONTAINS A SPLINTER OF WOOD FROM THE CROSS UPON WHICH JESUS WAS CRUCIFIED . ST. CONSTATINE AND HIS MOTHER ELENE ARE SHOWN ON ONE SIDE. THE OTHER HAS THE IMAGE OF JESUS. ST. ELENE FOUND THE CROSS.

BOUNCING MORTAR SHELL!

After leaving Tambak we were clearing out a small town close by. It was almost nighttime. I hated routing out the enemy at night when I couldn't see anything but blackness! We were going house to house searching every room, every closet, rifle at ready.

Slowly, carefully, I examined each area. I went into the peoples' bedroom. There is no one there (we often wondered where these people went when we would occupy their homes — taking them over, eatin their food, drinking their wine and sleeping on those marvelous down-stuffed pillows).

Suddenly there was a crash at the window to my left. A mortar shell had come through, breaking the glass. It hit the floor not more than five feet from me. It bounced all about the room exactly like a ping pong ball bounces.

It did not explode. Again, my wonderful, sweet maternal grandmother had come to Piff's salvation protected by her gold religious amulet.

SPIRITS!..BOOZE!...FREE AND POTENT!!

One gorgeous crisp April day heading towards Saalfield, Germany, we came upon a scene in a village that I will never forget. Normally the German civilians tolerated us but were generally polite and considerate. There was certainly no joy upon seeing us. After all, this was war, and we were the enemy.

Now imagine this scene, a large, red, brick, three story building sitting on a corner of this cobblestone street. The left and front has been partially demolished by artillery. There was a large sign on the building hanging askew that appeared to have a large picture of a bottle of wine, or beer on it with German wording. Apparently, indicating the building's purpose, a warehouse of stored spirits. There is loud talking and laughing going on by lots and lots of people. We stood staring down, at the top of a hill, wondering what the hell was going on.

People, old and young joyously happy, are going in and out carrying all types of containers filled with some sort of liquid. Apparently, our artillery barrage had hit the building causing the contents to break. The contents were spirits!

What sticks in my mind today, is that of an elderly lady wearing the garments of a farmer's wife standing ankle deep in this liquid, gently and slowly dipping a garden water can—the kind with a long spout—sideways, into this lake of mixed booze. At times she would take a break by dipping a glass jar into the "pool" and partaking of a swig on the spot.

I watched her and a fine looking old gentleman, he carefully manipulating/carrying a full, metal bucket, happily sloshing through the liquid up some steps and out onto those cobblestones.

It wasn't long before all of us, enemy and conquerors were sloshed, consuming a mixture of every type of—we guess—bourbon, vodka, brandy, wine—who knows, but it was, well, it was very effective. The next day, we named the town Hangover, Germany.

"TANKS" FOR HELPING US ROB A BANK

I remember when we rolled into the suburbs of Tambak, Germany in a beautiful quaint little village in late spring of 1945. Sitting in the middle of an immaculate square was a small, elegant bank with a Doric façade—a glorious structure, all marble! The two front doors were brass and massive, maybe 12 or 14 feet tall. They were locked tight.

We had to clear it of any enemy, but how to do it with those heavy doors? Someone had a bright idea. Crash through them not with a hand grenade but with the might of the vaunted Sherman tank! So, that's what we did.

The tank rumbled forward with all the clanking, chain created noises, massive and terrifying but to us beautiful and slowly approached the doors. The cannon turned towards the rear, looking like a javelin that was set to go backwards. Slowly the tank ground forward, pushing the massive doors open. It continued on the inside.

Now imagine an American tank inside of a bank, marble floors, marble customer tables, offices located on the sides of a perimeter separated by beautiful carved, decorative, partitions. The tank stopped. With the driver standing out of the turret, the cannon slowly revolved around and around, ready to eliminate any enemy. None were there.

Now the challenge was how to open the giant, beautifully decorated vault. The use of a shell from the cannon would be too devastating so we called in the bazooka boys. That worked! We swung the doors open and found mountains of German currency. The explosion wreaked havoc among the items inside but everything else was still intact. We stuffed our pockets full of all this money, becoming "rich" overnight. We had found oodles of German Marks before which were useless except when we ran out of toilet paper. It had no value except for that.

One of my best friends, Al Fahey, walked over to me and said, "Piff, I got a present for you." He presented me with a beautiful P-38 pistol, which he had gotten off some fancy dressed officer, either a colonel or general. He also relieved this officer of his watch, which was standard procedure. I had been looking for either a Luger or P-38 for months and now I had one thanks to my buddy Al.

That is the first and last time I had ever been involved in "robbing" a bank.

ENGINEERS! BLOW UP THIS ROAD BLOCK!

The war began grinding to a halt. We were moving so rapidly we did not have the time for the kitchen to catch up with us. We were living off of K-rations and C-rations. As usual Dutch Kulenkamp, my best friend, and I were selected to be the point for the battalion. (The "point" is the name given to the soldiers that were the first of any procession of troops as they moved forward). Many times I regretted my bragging of being a Major in ROTC at Tech High school in Atlanta. The "point" was my reward.

We were going down a dirt road about 150 yards in front of the whole battalion moving at night not being able to see a damn thing. So we "parked" our young German prisoners in front of us as body shields.

It was now about 2:00 in the morning, and we were worn out. We then came to a massive roadblock perfectly situated at a very tight curve in the road. I was standing looking forward past the roadblock. Dutch was looking back towards the forthcoming engineers that we had just yelled for. Our two young prisoners were along side of us.

Suddenly, the night shone bright orange, yellow, and red, accompanied by gigantic explosion after explosion. Panzer tanks had opened up on us point blank firing through the roadblock. I flew 60 feet through the air back towards our company (it was dreamlike, almost like being in slow motion). I was surrounded, encompassed by flaming pieces of shrapnel resembling giant, yellow, flaming fire flies.

I fell flat on my stomach and bounced. Tully, our squad leader, yelled, "Piff, are you hurt?"

I replied rather laconically, "No, Tully, just bounced on my stomach. I've got a sore belly." He later remarked that he'd never heard of anybody being so cool before. Tully never knew how terrified I was. I was just trying not to show my fear.

Dutch had disappeared, as had the two prisoners. One was hanging high in a tree, badly injured screaming, calling for his mother jabbering in German. German sounds were heard on the other side of the roadblock, with questioning voices wondering what had happened. Had they fired on their own people?

In a short time, human sounds, the moaning and crying, had ceased. We settled down for the night.

At dawn, I volunteered to go find Dutch or—what was left of him. I circled an outcrop of very large granite boulders and peeked over the side. I looked down upon the scene of six or seven German tanks with soldiers sitting on them eating breakfast. It was impossible for me to do anything. I could not move without being seen.

Reluctantly, sadly, I went back and reported the situation to the Major. He gave the order and our artillery took over. For the next hour we blasted the place.

I knew Dutch was gone, a fantastic guy, always smiling, always cool, always funny, identified by his signature, wearing his helmet slightly cocked to the right.

Our barrage ended. The roadblock had been blown away. We began moving forward. Just at that moment who should come walking up, but Dutch Kulenkamp. His helmet sitting slightly to the right, that perpetual smile on his face was still there. On his left shoulder where you would pin an American Flag insignia was a little red spot a trickle of blood showing. That was his only wound.

All of us gathered around yelling and hugging him knowing that he had survived not only the initial German fire but also the unbelievable round after round of our artillery barrage.

Here is what happened. "Piff, when the shells hit the logs, I flew forward towards the Germans."

I said, "I flew backwards towards our guys."

He continued, "I fell flat on my stomach luckily into a dry creek bed. There were pebbles under me. Even with that racket, I could hear the Germans nearby, but I managed to get my body lower in the bed by removing large numbers of pebbles under me.

"When daylight came, Jerrys walked close by, assuming I was dead. No one touched me. I just lay there quietly, barely breathing.

"After a while all hell broke loose. I mean, really! You guys think that a bunch of incoming 88s is bad. Man, you guys ain't heard nothing until you have been shot at by your own artillery.

"Round after round after round hit close to me. My God, how am I going to survive this? Shells were exploding everywhere. I expected at any minute to just disappear off the face of the earth.

"Finally—finally—*finally* it stopped. Thank God, I'm still alive. I lay there quietly, not moving a muscle. The tanks had moved out as the barrage started."

Talk about being happy—we were ecstatic. Later, Dutch walked over to me and says, "Piff, tell YaiYai that she has another grandson whose name is Dutch. Dutch will always stick with Piff through hell and high water because where Piff is, apparently God goes too.

This young soldier is 13 years old. Our two soldiers we captured were about 15. Sadly, they were both killed in this action.

MISSION WITH A STRANGE LIEUTENANT

It was Easter morning in April 1945. Someone suggested we put a flower in our helmets to celebrate which we did. We were back away from the front sort of lolling around.

A new first lieutenant had just joined our company. He was with Eisenhower's headquarters at SHAEF (Supreme Headquarters American Expeditionary Forces). Lt. Big Shot was a handsome guy and he knew it. He bragged about what a tough job he had at SHAEF—yeah, we thought, "In Paris, with SHAEF, right! Now that is one tough job." His ambition though was to get a Combat Infantry Badge which was and is today one of the most coveted medals an infantryman can earn and wear. It is about 4 inches long, about ½ inch wide, with an embossed silver rifle in a blue background.

We had gotten the word out that the small hill in front of us was full of SS troupers (SS was the abbreviated way of identifying the elite guard that evolved as the "Protective Echelon" for the Nazi Party. In German SS means Schutzstaffel. Our not having been told to go there we just let them stay there. Well, Lt. Bigshot decided he wanted to become a hero. So with our flowers in our helmets he volunteered us to "wipe out those damn SS troupers."

Our Top Sergeant spoke to him in a nice way, saying that he did not think it was such a good idea. The lieutenant persisted though, so what do you do? We took off going up toward the hill. It was densely wooded. We were being quiet as hell, watching every shadow, rifles at ready. Our BAR guy, Josh, a wizened, Daniel Boone type from Kentucky, hated being in the Army and anyone in authority, particularly officers. He was, though, a good soldier whom we all respected.

As we got halfway up the hill, negotiating all the trees, making almost no noise, the Lieutenant shouts out for the world to hear something like "Come out you sons-of-bitches. We're ready for you!" We looked at him like he had lost his frigging mind! Everybody dropped to the ground, the chorus of whispered words telling him to be quiet—including, "SHUT UP, Lieutenant!" He replied, saying "What's wrong with you men? I thought you were soldiers! Why are you so damn afraid? Let's go get those bastards."

Josh, our ol' Kentucky buddy, the BAR man, went right up to him and whispered, "Lieutenant, you're going to shut that F'ing mouth of yours, or I am going to shoot your ass right now. Understand that, Lieutenant? No one will ever know the difference. Right, men?"

"Right!" We all whispered.

He turned white, started to say that he could not be talked to like that. He looked and saw all of our rifles pointed at him. As he walked back towards the place we came from, Josh said, "Lieutenant, this never happened, did it?" Lieutenant Big Shot said nothing but we knew he had gotten the message.

THE PRESIDENT, MR. ROOSEVELT WAVED AT ME!

April 12, 1945, we received notice that President Roosevelt had died in Warm Springs, Georgia. We had seen death many times, but this hit us as if we had lost an old uncle or grandfather. We all felt it.

I had found a camera in a farmhouse and had taken some pictures. I had no idea whether the any of the film was still unexposed. There was unexposed film; one picture shows a building with the flag flying at half mast.

The Greek immigrant had a special fondness for President Roosevelt. My father was one of the most ardent supporters of his presidency.

One day when I was about 12 years old, we had heard that he was heading again to Warm Springs. Somehow Dad knew his route through Atlanta. He took me and my two sisters to go to see "The Mr. President, if possible." We did. His open Ford convertible came around a corner close to the Marietta Bakery near West End. We all stood right at the curb. I can see him now. He was hatless, sitting straight up in the back. I waved as hard as I could. I went home yelling to my mother that "Mr. Roosevelt looked right at me and waved!" He did…to my 12-year-old eyes.

This picture was taken on 4-13-45, the day after President Roosevelt had died. Although barley discernable, our flag is flying at half mast. I do not remember the function of the large building, but a clue may be the parked vehicle bearing a red cross on its side i.e. an "ambulance".

YOU ARE READING SHAKESPEARE AND CHICKENS!

Top Sergeant, Walter J. Silva, besides being our platoon leader, was a brilliant young man. He had attended Harvard for a short while prior to being drafted. Walter was unique in many ways.

We all marveled at his ability to get things done in a way most advantageous to him. Somehow or another he had managed to finagle a backpack that was standard issue for use in jungle warfare. Ours was rather abbreviated in its configuration and did a good job. His could be described as being like a very large bag hanging over his shoulders down to his hips. This in no way lessened his ability to get around. It is beyond my knowledge at this point in life to remember how Walter did this. Nevertheless, in that big sack were several tomes; some were Shakespeare and other authors of note.

I remember on a few occasions when we were together behind the front, he and I would gather together under his "tent" (made up of our raincoats) and he would read out loud excerpts from these books. Our light source was a cigarette lighter, about the size of a small book, which he had liberated from an office somewhere.

I relished those moments. They removed me from the reality at hand. I was transported back to Atlanta, my hometown, being at the Carnegie Library looking for and reading anything I could.

Walter had a fetish for guns and pistols. Besides being adorned as all of us were with bandoleers of ammunition, Walter had pistols hanging all over his body.

He had one for chickens, one for the enemy, and one for just destroying these glorious six foot high vases that many of the finer German homes had in their parlors (when you shot one the correct way, it shattered in to a million pieces).

One bright glorious day early in May 1945 we stopped at a little small village. We took over the homes and happily the sleeping quarters, but stayed on the alert.

We had gotten so tired of rations that Walter said he would get us a chicken for supper. It was a farm area. There was livestock and chickens everywhere. One thing the farmers did in Germany was creating compost heaps made of animal and human waste and straw. This mixture would ferment steam evolving in the early morning from the fermentation. When properly cured, it was spread over the fields prior to planting. Sometimes it seemed as if grass was growing on the top, too.

This one little farm where the chickens roamed free had a large compost heap butting against a very small hill. I can see Walter now, running everywhere chasing this on chicken, trying to get close enough to shoot it in the head — damn hard to do. This went on for about five minutes with all of us guffawing in the back. It really was a hilarious sight.

Suddenly the chicken ran up the little knoll and over to the top of the compost heap, followed closely by Walter. You guessed it — Walter sank right in. Down he went in all that mess. He emerged disgusted and cursing possibly more because of our laughter than the way he stank and looked.

Walter's chicken pistol is probably still there at the bottom of that compost heap after all these years.

TWO YOUNG DISPLACED PERSONS...GIRLS!

In late April, 1945, we had stopped at a hill, pulled back from the lines and told to "Dig in!" So began the arduous job of digging a fox hole. It was really a chore! The shovel was small. It was hinged so you could turn a round collar to allow the handle to get horizontal with the shovel. You'd dig down and inevitably hit rocks or roots. Man, what a pain that was. I had gotten sort of jades. "Damn, the hell with it!" I would often say, and just dig as far as I could and give up and take my chances.

Now Geoff, a great guy from Arkansas, was about 40 years old, had a wife, three children and was very cautious, never took any chances. Man did he dig fox holes! We could have stopped and Ol' Geoff would still be digging. I was never his fox hole buddy. He managed to always get one that was as much a digger as he was. It worked. He got home without a scratch.

So, back on the hill, someone calls, "Hey Greek, come on up here. There are two Greek girls here you ought to meet."

"Two Greek girls? What the hell is he talking about?"

I walk up towards these two young women, each carrying a beat up suitcase. One says to the other in Greek, "Af toes then tha eennay Ellinas. Axee galena matia (This guy cannot be Greek, he has blue eyes)!" I replied in Greek that there were lots of blue-eyed Greeks. Overcome with surprise, they started talking and laughing excitedly. They had been taken from their homes when they were fourteen and fifteen a few years before, and forced to work in Nazi aircraft factories. They babbled in Greek how they had tried to do what they could to be as inefficient as possible. In fact, one volunteered that they knew of friends who worked at munitions factories that managed to make rounds that would not explode (probably like the 80 mm artillery shell that failed to explode at my feet as we crossed the Rhine River).

They had been used with every meaning of that word. They looked it. They subsisted on a bowl of soup for lunch and a hunk of bread for dinner. They showed me their dog-eared ration booklets which they were keeping to show their "mbaba" and "mymy," father and mother, when they would get home.

Margarita Takasova, the elder one, was very bright and spoke a little French, Polish, Italian, and of course, German and Greek. The other girl,

Vasiliki Kouloura only spoke German and Greek. Their home town in Greece was Kalimno.

I had, as we all did, lots of German marks on us. I took out a handful and handed them to them. Vasiliki asked, "What are we to do with these, use them for toilet paper?" They were worthless.

I gave them some rations and cigarettes and wished them on their way. Margarita stopped just before leaving and asked me, "Pes mou? Pos les, sey 'agape' Angleeka (Tell me? How do you say, 'I love you' in English)?" I told her. I suppose these young ladies had really been used.

(As I have stated before, I did not keep a log of my experiences. The reason that I can relate these facts in such detail is because they were written in a letter that I sent my sister, Evelyn. She included this in a column that she wrote in a magazine with which she was a frequent writer.)

THE CALVADOS CAPER

In mid November of 1944 we arrived in France and bivouacked in Normandy, pup tents all lined up in an apple orchard, cold and raining for days, misery incarnate. Our Executive Officer Wells with whom I had a tenuous connection (he was from Cape Cod and had graduated from Harvard where I had been a freshman) asked me how my French was. I had three years in high school taught by a French Canadian in what she claimed was French and one semester in College. I told him it was rudimentary. He thought that was enough. We were in Calvados country and he thought a shot of apple brandy would elevate company spirits. I was to take the company jeep and visit the farm a mile or so away, ask the farmer to sell us Calvados. He gave me an empty Jerry can to fill with the booze and ten dollars to pay for it. Easy, the farmer was very friendly (gushingly grateful for our presence) gave me a shot of the stuff and filled the Jerry can to the brim with his best. He didn't want the money, but I insisted the company was thrilled and lined up with their tin cups to be filled by the cook. Revelry was short-lived. Soon there was moaning and groaning and throwing-up throughout the company, only non-drinkers (including Lt. Wells and me) escaped. Wells took a sip of the booze. It turned out the Jerry can was not entirely empty of gas when the Calvados was added. Luckily it was apparently not enough to be fatal but the boys in the band were sick as dogs for a while.

THE JEEP CAPER . . . . "DAYLIGHT REQUISITION"
THE SIGNATURE OF THESE IS "W" WHO REQUESTED NO ATTRIBUTION

We went into reserve in a small farm village (I don't recollect after what activity). Our platoon occupied a small barn (Company HQ of course took over the farm house). We were supposed to get a week off including a chance for a shower and kitchen prepared meals. I think we were there two or three days (no shower and the cook heated up C-rations for us) when we were told we would be replaced and move up to the line. Our replacements arrived, in admirable military style, class A uniforms and neckties (the 76th- Liberty Bell Division). Their platoon lined up outside the barn. The Lieutenant went in and into a tirade. We were a disgrace to the army; dirty, messy, disorganized, etc. We left in the middle of his speech generally pissed off at the pompous ass...as we passed the farm house we saw a brand new jeep parked in front next to our somewhat disreputable company jeep. Joe Christopher (his real name was Christides) at 40+, the oldest guy in the Company, and I jumped in and took off not stopping till we were out of the village. We waited for the Platoon to catch up and everyone put his gear in the back and, unburdened, we all went on with the rest of the company. A little mud disguised the numbers on the bumpers and we kept the thing a week before questions arose and we left it by the side of the road.

W

LOOKING FOR TEENY GERMAN SOLDIERS

After all these years after the end of WWII, readers may wonder about certain aspects of how the American troops dealt with the civilian enemy.

In some of my stories you've read, I referred to the taking of German homes. This was a fact. We thought nothing of it. We were the conquerors. We had no idea where these people went when we took over a home, nor did we even think about it. Any item in a house was ours for the taking. Guys took—looted, not a negative word—all kinds of thing. Jewelry was the favorite to grab first before anyone else did.

Bill was our "designated" looter of watches (his family owned a watch repair store in Indiana). Bill had watches all over his body. He would take them off dead enemy soldiers. He had watches on both arms and in every pocket. Later, he would stash them somewhere to send home. He was also the least excitable guy in our squad (very "cool," in today's lingo).

One day, he and I were in a small town, checking out a house for any Jerrys. We were together in a bedroom. Bill goes right to the chest of drawers and starts rooting around in them. At that moment, in walks a lovely, tall woman in her forties and says in perfect English, "What, may I ask, are you doing there, young man?"

Without even a pause or looking up at this interloper, Bill answers, "Ma'am, I'm looking for little teeny German soldiers." She stormed out while I burst into laughter. He really was a cool guy.

Eventually, Bill lucked up when he found his "crown jewel" of watch making. His quest for a tiny watchmaker's lathe came to an end when he found one. "It's perfect!" It was sitting right out in the open, in a nice home, near Falkenstein, Germany.

MEMOIRS OF A PLATOON SERGEANT COMPANY G, 345TH REGIMENT, 87TH DIVISION, GENERAL PATTON'S 3RD ARMY

These are stories told me in Virginia on October 8th, 2008 at the home of my good friend and ex platoon sergeant, W.J.S. (Walt asked for no attribution.) He was and is a brilliant person. Boston born with a semester at Harvard prior to being drafted, he at the age of 19 led one of the platoons, ours, in our company.

He was 18, as were many of my colleagues that joined the company as replacement infantrymen. All were clueless, scared and dumb as blazes. Not Walt, rather short with a definite Massachusetts accent still possessed, commanded respect because of his maturity and intellect. One felt comfortable following his orders. Walt was also a nut about guns. He had several pistols all designated for a specific purpose. One was his "Vase pistol". Some of these vases were 6 feet tall and occupied a prominent place usually in a corner of the living room in some of the more ostentatious homes in which when on a few occasions "bivouacked". Walt just loved to stand a few feet back and take one shot into the middle of the vase. It would shatter in hundreds of pieces.

Walt was the intellectual giant in our battalion, no one carried heavy tomes in ones backpack. Walt did. There were times when he and I would share a foxhole. To keep the lights out, we'd cover ourselves with our raincoats, while he would read excerpts out loud. Our light source came from a giant cigarette lighter that he had liberated from a building somewhere.

Now as to guns, Walt was festooned with an assortment. The M 1 Garand rifle was standard issue to all of us. But somehow Walt would be seen "wearing" a Lugar, a 45 and or a M 1 Carbine, or cradling a M 3 Grease gun – one weird "Tommy Gun" that looked like the "gun" one uses to grease a car's parts – that's why the name. His massive backpack was not like the one we all wore. His was the standard issue for the Pacific theater! It was like a large canvass sack. It could hold all kinds of stuff (the tomes!) much more that the M 1 Haversack that was standard issue. We often wondered how he managed to scrounge that one up!

My favorite of his guns was his "Chicken gun." Right! "chicken," used sorely to execute chickens thereby providing his troops with fare other than the standard C and K rations type. He was a superb marksman taking aim at the creature's head at a full 3 to 4 inches.

On one beautiful day in the March '45, we were behind the lines enjoying the weather just before crossing the Mosel River. We were at a quaint little farm sitting on the grass under the trees. There were a few squawking chickens running around. Apparently, Walt had a hankering for some chicken. Out comes his trusty Lugar Chicken pistol. Then there began a hilarious race between man and animal. Walt was not to be denied his chicken supper, shot after shot rang out. Miss after miss prevailed. Finally as the quarry began to weaken, it ran up a slight incline to the top of this mound. (Now, understand that it was the custom of the German farmers at that time, to save and gather all human and animal waste to be used as fertilizer, an odiferous but worthwhile task. They combined the crap with straw creating a steaming compost heap.) Our chicken must have been aware of this fact, for it chose to run to the to of the hillock i.e. the compost heap followed by Walt, who by now was not to be denied his meal of and by this damn chicken.

You guessed it. Squawking chicken made it over the top and down the other side. Walt made it to the top and then disappeared into the "bowels" of the crap composting mess. We howled with laughter. Walt emerged shouting expletive after expletive using the word in which he was covered and smelling the same. There was no shower to take, no water to use to remove this shit. No wanting to "bother" our 'steamed leader, we all stayed away from him; we could not stand to be near him! The next day at the Mosel, Walt, managed to fall in the river prior to embarking thus cleansing himself of fresh manure.

(After the war, Walt graduated from Harvard, entered the diplomatic corps served all over the world distinguished himself earning many promotions and accolades.)

We were at "St Vith staying at this very picturesque little farm which included a small stable, as the 76th Division arrived or better sauntered into town. They looked as if they had stepped out of a Band box. Neat to a fault, class one uniforms, ties, pressed trousers, caps placed perfectly on newly haircutted heads. "Wow, what is this we thought?" (Our trucks remained there where we had parked. We thought that we were supposed to take the trucks for another unknown "journey". The lead lieutenant of the 76th parked his Jeep near them.)

As we watched these pristine troops march past us, we thought we heard them uttering insulting remarks about us. It was true, the officer in charge a first lieutenant, in a voice loud enough for us hear, was making remarks about what slobs we were. We had just returned from the field. What the hell did he expect us to look like! Also, we thought, they had yet to see combat . . "they'll find out we thought." That really pissed us off.

The lieutenant had parked his jeep near our trucks. "Well that was neat, we thought. He was such an asshole let's show him what we think about him and his "pristine troops". So we got in it and drove it away . . stole it! Our trucks were pulling out so we followed them happily in his Jeep; its back full of our packs . .heavy stuff.

It was 2 or 3 weeks later when the company commander caught up with us and our new Jeep. "How did you guys get that damn Jeep?" he asked. We explained. "Well get it back to him now!", he exclaimed! That was not too good because all of our packs were still in it. Now we had to get them out and carry them ourselves! After taking our stuff out, I drove around a curve in the woods and just left it there. Don't know if he ever found it!

The 76th made us look good. This was in early February,'45; we were still in Belgium, Companies G and E were up front, F, was in reserve. E went thru the town very quickly. Most of the Germans took off. When G moved in from one of the flanks, it looked like the town was clear. But it was not. Out came as usual, the local mayor with his paraphernalia around his neck identifying him as such and loudly proclaimed, "Welcome, welcome Americans so good to see you! Welcome! Thank you very much!

He continued whispering, saying, "There are still Germans here in our town. Most of them are in that house over there. I think they are having lunch" He pointed to a farm house about 100 yards away.

So we went there. I knocked on the door. The Germans had no clue that we were there. We knocked again. There was no answer. I was carrying a Grease gun, the poor man's Thompson, so I fired about 16 rounds into the door and the lock. We heard cries and screams coming from inside. We broke our way in found the Krauts sitting around a table eating. Up went their hands. They surrendered on the spot. I believe that they were the last bunch of Germans in St Vith.

(St Vith, in Belgium, was a crucial road junction. During the Battle of the Bulge, it was at the center of attacks and counterattacks by both forces. It suffered terrible destruction. That was the deadliest campaign of WWII. Americans suffered 19,000 men killed.)

St Vith, was the first town that I remember vividly. I will never forget the utter destruction that I witnessed. Trees reaped apart, houses with roofs and walls partially blown away, dead cows were strewn everywhere. One even was caught in the top branches of a large oak tree, legs held straight out, seemingly bloated to the point of bursting.

In January '45 Walt was the BAR man (Browning Automatic Rifle) which was sort of a machine gun , quite heavy at 21 pounds requiring also the wearing of 20 pounds of an ammo belt. It   was carried normally by a stalwart, strong individual. It would be fired in quick bursts, a great weapon but subject to jamming. Here one of the smallest men in the company, assigned as the BAR man. Weird!

Corporal Walt, brilliant as he was managed to get some else to be the BAR man and replaced that with a "found" again, Grease gun, the M 3.

A few weeks later, this new corporal was running a platoon as a noncom of the highest rank, a top sergeant! That is when I met him.

For some reason when Walt took over our platoon it became the repository of some of the odd ball characters, troubled soldiers that would surface at times. No one knew what to do with them. They landed in our platoon.

One of them was Elio Crecco from New York City. His was a strange saga. Elio, a tourist, was caught in the States when the war broke out. Walt, "and like an idiot, he enlisted. He was a great guy, as nice as they come, a good, good person, honestly patriotic! But he spoke only about 20 words of English, that's about it! So I being the recognized "linguist of the battalion, spoke a little French, was awarded Elio."

"Remember that horrendous bombardment with bullets and shells flying everywhere from 88's, burp guns, machine guns? We were dug in at the edge of the woods. The Germans were at the end of the meadow?" I said, "Yes." "Well, Elio, was in his foxhole with his buddy, another odd ball, an Englishman. A direct hit by an 88 shell killed them both. (The Englishman, Edgar, enlisted in the American Army, to get his citizenship.) The company commanders could not communicate with them so they wound up with me."

Then Walt asked me if I remember the American Indians that were in our company, I did not. *"Well, one was Alesandro Barsuto, the other Simon Flores. They spoke a little English, great buddies. Flores was a Navajo, Flores, a Pima. I heard that the tribes were enemies at home but these two guys were bosom buddies. They both survived the war."*

My parents emigrated from Greece in the early 1900's. Walt spent several years as the American representative for the U.S. in Salonika. So we have a Greek connection.

He spoke very kindly of Joe Christopher (Christoforides) of Wilkes-Barrie, PA. *"Joe was an old man, I was 19 and he was 48. I don't know why he did it, but he wanted to be in the Army and he was.*

In late January '45, it had snowed quite a bit. We were struggling thru the snow. The mine sweepers had been called in to clear the area of mines which they did. But stupidly they cleared the roads not where we were walking in the woods and fields. Poor Joe and a friend out in the woods tripped a bouncing "Betty" bomb. They were both killed instantly. I was not aware that it had happened as we left the woods, but I do remember hearing an explosion.

About six weeks later, the squad leader of Graves registration asked me if might have been in some woods – he described them as, "a while back". I said I thought so. He said they had found several dead soldiers that had been buried in the snow now melting. So I went there and sure enough it was Joe and his buddy their bodies frozen in the exact position as when they died. What a shame, I thought. He was great guy, a very kind *sweet person*.

I asked the Graves guy, "Why in hell did you come all the way over here to learn who these men were. All you had to do was look at their dog tags!" He said, 'Oh, we don't want to get that close to them." Can you believe that?"

The Battle of the Bulge.

Walt. *"It was the coldest time on record, down to below zero at times. Man, we were cold as hell. Two men on guard were found frozen to death in their sitting position. (Grotesquely, that is how they lay at the Graves registration site, lying on their sides in a sitting position.)*

We arrived on Christmas Day took our position on the side of a hill an area that the Krauts had just left where they had built these fancy, fancy bunkers out of logs dug into the hill with log roofs. Very comfortable quarters for our company commander while the troops had to dig foxholes in solid ice, solid ice! The ground was frozen so hard, that we had to use a grenade to make a foxhole. A lot of people lost toes and some feet from the frost bite.

As to what we wore, everybody did about the same thing. You put on both suits that you had the fatigues, the wool pants, two shirts, a field jacket, then the overcoat and a raincoat the whole bunch. Then you took the fart sack over the

(It was a sleeping bag made of G.I, blanket wool. We would make holes for the arms and then cut the bottom off.) *It went over everything. By the time you got thru, you could barely move. Even with all of that you were still cold. Then we had those stupid shoes."*

I too remember how cold it was when I arrived there in February. We were frozen. One of the senior men I first met, Albert Persiante, took his glove off, held his open faced palm to me where I could see it closely. All of his fingers had little star figures on the tips from being chapped caused by the exposure to such cold. They would bleed at the slightest pressure. Extremely painful!

Walt:

"The first action with our Division (the 87th) was at the Maginot Line in France. Our Regiment, (the 345th) was ordered to take Metz. There were these enormous WWI fortresses there.

We suffered the first casualty for our Company (G) there. This happened to be one of the "back home" cadre guys. He was tall, had played quarterback for Boston College. We heard him yell, "I've been hit!". He was standing leaning against a tree holding his upper arm which was bleeding profusely.

We wondered how that had happened not having heard any small arms fire at that moment. He had shot himself, yep "accidentally".

Within a day and a half, a dozen ex cadre men had done the same thing, shot themselves. This included our ol'-tough-as-nails-cadre-Top Sarg, his self! He put a bullet into his foot!

Before long ALL of the old cadre guys were either sick or had shot themselves or something, all gone!

That is how my friend Walt, 19 years old, a private in December '44 was promoted to a top sergeant two months later when I got there, a platoon leader of about 40 men.

BEER BARREL POLKA...GERMAN STYLE

I have always been impressed at how my colleagues of the 87th Division in writing articles for the 87th Association magazine, "GAN," have been able to remember specific towns in which we fought. They remember even some of the roads. Piff—that's me—was so clueless, and apparently I still am. I could not remember many of those places or their names. Nevertheless, one beautiful April day in 1945, we were ensconced in a beautiful quaint Bavarian village with streets that were very unique. They were made out of cobblestones—nice, rounded, well worn, handsome cobblestones.

It was a hilly area. We had difficulty walking around, particularly on these cobblestone streets. Luckily, two of us had the most expensive room at our "hotel" with a great view of the small town, particularly these quaint cobblestone streets.

About 10:00 in the morning, I heard a racket that I couldn't identify. It was a noise interspersed with cheers or screams or maybe laughter and the rattling and bouncing sounds of things seemingly rolling down this cobblestone street.

Al Fahey, my good buddy who was the oldster of our squad, about 30—I was 19, looked out the window with me.

Down the hill on this beautiful, crisp, sunshiny day came a bunch of GIs screaming, laughing, yelling, and happily following a cascade of five metal drums of beer. These were careening down this cobblestone street, bouncing off any obstacle, going into front yards, trees, fronts of houses, on their way down, helter skelter.

At the bottom of the hill where they were captured, there was a celebration, but one with consternation. The first thing, how do we open these damn things? Second, when opened, will they explode?

Well, leave it to good old GI ingenuity. In concert with a giant spray of beer they opened them up, the guys trying to guzzle even the spray. It ended with everyone drunk, at times swapping with their peers, liquid from one barrel to the other, creating their own half-and-half potions.

MAN! LET ME SHOWER MYSELF WITH PERFUME!

One of my good friends in our platoon was Tony Barbuto. He was about 5'8", slightly rotund, proud of his appearance and particularly how he smelled.

Tony was very fastidious. He despised being dirty and not taking a shower every day.

His solution was to apply liberally any concoction of nice smelling liquid he could find. There was usually a pretty good supply of this stuff because many times we stayed in peoples' homes. I can see ol' Tony now, routing around in the cabinets and bedrooms and acquiring any kind of perfume he could find.

Some had wonderful fragrances, while others were not too appealing and sort of stank. Nevertheless, Tony would adorn himself with these liquids and happily go through his function of being a combat infantryman.

In reality, some of us objected to Tony smelling so good. If we could detect him from a few hundred feet away, so could the enemy. He disregarded our admonishments; he just kept on doing it, his philosophy being, "If I can't take a bath every day and I don't like the way I smell, then I will smell like I want to smell by putting perfume on me.

To best describe tony, is to think of those World War II movies in which there is always this smart aleck, bright, usually good-looking, Italian kid from Brooklyn. He would disdain with amusement and look down upon Army regulations, but he would always comport himself with humor. That was Tony.

Our top sergeant was a typical D.I. Sgt. Hess was tall and ramrod in appearance and demeanor. He brooked no nonsense from anyone. He was a good man, knew what he was talking about, and expected to be listened to and his orders carried out immediately and specifically.

Hess and Barbuto were like mixing sodium and water. They just plain did not interact too happily.

One eventful day we had moved back from the front lines to the rear and took over homes in this beautiful little village to recuperate. As usual, Tony was not around. Hess called out in a loud voice, "Barbuto! Has anyone seen

Barbuto?" We all looked at each other with raised eyebrows, thinking that guy is probably rummaging around in somebody's bedroom trying to find some more perfume.

This went on for many minutes, maybe up to fifteen. By now Hess was seeing blood. "Where in the hell is that damn Italian? That son-of-a-bitch is gonna drive me crazy!" were the words uttered under his breath. Finally here comes ol' Barbuto, sauntering over, happy as could be whistling carrying a nice large bottle of perfume he just liberated. This inflamed Sgt. Hess. He went ballistic. "God damn it Barbuto, where in the hell have you been you son of a bitch? Come here!" Barbuto walks over to him, his 5'8" frame somewhat slouched, his head down, looking at his feet, his belly poking out slightly. All of us watching felt that Barbuto was not about to yield to the system.

The harangue lasted for at least three minutes. Every four letter word, every expletive Hess could muster was directed towards a downcast Barbuto. Of his closest friends, I was one of those that called him Barbeauty because he was so "beautiful" and smelled so good.

After Hess ran out of words, his face red with excitement and frustration, he directed one last comment to Barbuto and said, "Well, what the hell do you have to say for yourself, Barbuto?"

Slowly Barbuto lifted his head towards the sergeant, who stood at least six inches taller, put his face near Hess', smiled and said, "Tiss me, Sargy!" Talk about going ballistic! Hess just stood there flustered, mumbled cuss words, and walked away. The rest of us were on the floor guffawing. That was our boy, Barbuto. We loved him.

THAT'S OL' BARBUTO (BARBEAUTY) SECOND FROM LEFT!

STOP PLAYING WITH THAT RIFLE! IT'LL....OOPS!

I remember the first time as a replacement combat infantryman I experienced sleeping in other peoples' homes.

My first few nights in Belgium were spent with a machine gun crew on top of a hill witnessing a barrage going both ways over our heads.

Magically the next night we were ensconced in a beautiful small home, two stories, well kept, perfectly clean, well stocked with food.

My new buddy Al and I marked one of the bedrooms as our spot to sleep—on my God a luxurious soft wonderful bed! But these beds were different. I do not know why the German people favored these very, very large down-filled pillows. They were about the size of the mattress. Nevertheless, it was luxurious comfort.

This time my old buddy Kuntz had migrated to our bedroom—we don't know why. He was just sitting on the floor cleaning his Garand.

The rest of the guys of our whole squad were in the kitchen at about 9:00 at night. We had made some hot chocolate using the chocolate bars and some milk from a nearby cow that gave it to us happily (all of us got diarrhea the next day). We were enjoying a nice night inside a warm home. Freddy, a new recruit who was sort of a klutz was next to me sitting on the floor cleaning his rifle. He kept doing something very disturbing to all of us: he kept putting in the cartridge and clicking it out. Sgt Tully, our squad leader, said, "Freddy, get that damn cartridge out, or you are going to kill somebody." No sooner had he said that than the trigger was pressed, the gun was pointed straight up, and a round went off with a big explosion. It went through the ceiling to the second floor and missed Kuntz' butt by about two inches. The wags (and we had several in that squad) were giggling because we all perceived Kuntz as being an asshole. Had Freddy found his mark, he would have had two of them.

WALK BACKWARD WHILE PEEING—NO WAY!

As a combat infantryman, one of the things that worried us more besides getting killed was to keep lice off. Another was to have a lot of toilet paper and manage to perform your hygienic functions quickly so one would not be left behind—no pun intended, and to have a good supply of cigarettes.

As for the lice, we all had a can of DDT on us. I sacrificed one of the sections for my ammo belt to house a can of this powder. I would douse myself completely each day. It worked, and I never had any lice.

The toilet paper came in little brown rolls about the size of a fat lipstick case. We sort of mashed them down to where they became rather oblong, allowing them to fit perfectly in your helmet's headliner. I walked around "festooned" with hidden toilet paper on my head.

For the hygienic moments doing number two, required a quick run to the bushes, pulling off all your outer wear, belts, exposing your bottom, doing a quick dump, wiping yourself quickly and then catching up with your buddies. You never wanted to be too far away from your squad as they trudged through the woods.

Number one—peeing—also took time and doing, making you rush to catch up with your friend. Those of us that were skilled at this function developed what we referred to as the "Backass Method." Although hard to do, with a little concentration and effort and the concurrence of the guy behind you, you peed walking backwards. Most of us got quite skilled at doing it.

The only time peeing backward didn't work is when you were in a truck. You couldn't pee. You were jammed with 50 other guys. The truck would be going down the road helter skelter, bouncing up and down, hitting every pothole. You had one heck of a time just keeping your bottom on the seat if you were lucky enough to have one. After a while when you had to pee, almost in unison, there would be a loud piss call coming from all the guys. It always amazed me. It seemed like it was a programmed call. The trucks would move to the side and park. Everybody would jump out, run over the side of the road and start peeing. It reminded me of a bunch of birds sitting on a telephone wire, all nicely lined up doing their thing.

One night, the trucks would not stop, now even for piss call. We didn't know where we were going but we traveled for hours. Well something had to give. One of the guys got the bright idea. He took his helmet off, relieved himself and passed it around to his neighbors. Each one made his contribution.

The helmet was passed around somewhat like one does passing a hot dog to a neighbor at a football game. The guy at the end would gingerly pour it out the back. We laughed about it but took it seriously. No one wanted to get wet by this well mixed and unidentified urine.

This would go on despite the bumps and bouncing of the truck, everyone gingerly watching the helmets to they would not fill up too much then passing them to the guys at the back.

Well, you guessed it. As ol' Billy Bob, a friend from Georgia, carefully and gingerly received the receptacle for dispersal, the truck took one hell of a bounce. Poor Billy Bob got really pissed—and pissed on—and pissed off at our howls of laughter. He was drenched wet! We were drenched with laughter.

THE 88 SHELL LANDED AT OUR FEET!

We had just crossed the Rhine River and were pinned down by an 88 Battery sitting on a rise. The terrain was such that we were readily exposed. Frustrated, our company commander, Lt. Coats, asked for volunteers to eliminate it. Three of us took the challenge, Walter J. Silva, Dutch Kulenkamp and I.

Under Walter's superb leadership, we managed to keep out of the sight of the battery by crawling at the shoreline sometimes in the water. We made good progress.

Around a curve was about 100 yards space of land we had to cross with no brush or cover. The 88 continued firing at our company—still pinned down. Walter looked at the situation and said, "When I say go, run like hell!"

After a crescendo of shells hit the company area, Walter yelled, "Go!" and we took off running like our life depended upon it (which it did).

As we sprinted towards a tall forest of trees, the Jerrys turned the 88 towards us and let loose a shell. It screamed at us—that eerie sound that terrified us all—and it hit—at our feet! I mean, not more than 2 feet from us, but it did not explode!

We flew towards the trees hidden by their superb foliage. Carefully, slowly, we climbed the small, steep hill. We managed to circle their position undetected. There were four men there commanded by a handsome young officer. He was meticulously groomed even down to a flowing grey cape.

It was no contest. It was over in a few moments. They had no idea what hit them (Walter received a Silver Star).

What sticks in my mind today—I'll never forget it—is the look on Walter's and Dutch's, and mine, too, I guess, at the sight of that shell hitting the ground making a hole within inches of our bodies and not exploding. My wonderful grandmother's religious gold amulet taped to my chest helped save us.

K-RATION CHEESE WITH A MIND OF ITS OWN!

It was towards the end of the war, and we were confronted time after time with roadblocks. Because of not much resistance, Lt. Coates decided for us to stop to spend the night in a grove of woods.

Nothing was unusual about that except for some reason which none of us understood, we stopped and made do, on the side of a hill the slope of which must have been 45 degrees!

It was almost impossible to stand or walk. One had to balance one's self to counteract gravity. Thick young stands of pine trees gave some measure of security. You could not fall down this hill. The trees would stop you!

The average diameter of these pine trees was about 6 inches with the foliage beginning about 8 feet high.

We slept. It was rather easy, two hours on, two hours off. I had a hard time keeping my eyes open on my watch because being in the sitting position I was in effect lying down at a 45 degree angle.

The next morning we were awakened to the sound of motors starting and the clanky, grinding, distinctive noise of German tanks within a few hundred feet.

Fortunately, the stand of trees' growth at the height tended to obscure the tanks from us and vice versa. We sat there very quietly, having our breakfast—a breakfast of canned beans and K rations or a chocolate bar.

I selected K rations that contained a tin of cheese about 3 inches in diameter. Slowly, carefully, quietly I removed the top of the can with my fingers and removed the cheese. It slipped! Being in the sitting position in which I was, almost lying down, I had a hard time trying to catch it, and I couldn't. Dutch was about 3 meters in front o me. I whispered to him, "Dutch, grab that cheese!"

Dutch didn't help a bit. By the time he turned to see what was going on, the cheese went right by him. Now imagine a hunk of cheese shaped like a small wheel, yellow in color, snaking itself down the slope. It missed every pine tree it could. It was amazing. The whole squad sat there wide-eyed, watching this cheese as if it had a life of its own, going straight down towards the bottom of the slope into the waiting arms of our enemy!

(You are reading this but you don't believe it, do you? I swear, it happened exactly as they described.)

We craned our necks to see where it was going. As it got towards the bottom of the hill, there was a lessening of the slope to a nice smooth flatness.

It rolled and rolled. It went down the slope into a flat area and exactly under the first tank.

No one said a word. We just looked at each other, eyes wide and frightened. Dutch said to me, "Piff, if they find that damn cheese you son-of-a-gun, we are all dead. They can turn that machine gun turret around and wipe us out. We can barely stand up, let alone run!" They could have!

Luckily fate decreed that we would not die a "cheesey" death.

A few moments later, the rumble, clanking, incredible noise of tanks taking off and moving, proceeded with tank after tank moving over my cheese, straddling it perfectly.

About an hour later I retrieved my breakfast with my bayonet, dusted off the leaves and dirt, and ate it.

HARD TO BELIEVE…SHAMEFUL!!

I believe the date was April 10th 1945. We were dug in outside of Tambac—a destroyed large city near Czechoslovakia, and it was a glorious warm day. I was sitting against a tree writing a letter home, my helmet beside me with a small flower in the netting, indicative of our wish to be home for the Easter holidays. It was one of these nice, normal days which we enjoyed now and then.

Appearing out of nowhere came an excited Chon—I believe that was his name—saying, "Piff, come with us, we are gonna kill a bunch of Germans."

I looked at him with an amused look, saying, "Hell, man, that's what we have been doing, what are you talking about?"

"No, man," he continued, "We captured about 15 of these guys, and no one wants to trek them back to the rear as prisoners. We are moving so damn fast we are just gonna shoot their asses. I know that Germans have killed some of our prisoners, so we are going to kill some of theirs, too."

I could not believe what I was hearing! "You have got to be kidding, Chon, man you got to be nuts. You can't go around killing prisoners like that."

He countered, "You want to take them back?"

"Hell, yeah, I will take them back if you are serious. I don't give a shit man, I've got my weapon, they don't have theirs. Hell, I'll take them back. I don't give a damn, I don't kill people. That would be insane."

He looked at me with disgust and took off. In all honesty I was not a witness to any of this. I did not hear gunshots. There was sporadic shooting going on all the time everywhere, so I didn't notice anything different.

Then the word got out. "Did you hear about that, guys, about the third battalion? I think it was Company G, killed a bunch of prisoners outright." I almost vomited. "This can't be true," I said to myself, "It can't be true!" Unfortunately, it was. It was sickening.

Now let's fast forward to 2003. An incredible young man, James Bramswig jr., son of John Bramswig, who was in Company F, of the 345th, has been a strong supporter and advocate o the 87th Division Association and its history in World War II. John has done a great amount of research about this situation. He sent me barely discernable copies of the paper making this assertion.

It is marked SECRET at the top and at the bottom. It lists the names in alphabetical order of the men in G company. Most names have a small check mark, mine included. The perpetrators do not. The date is 12th April, 1945. The signature at the bottom right is that of our company commander, Lt. Robert C. Coats.

I was impressed that there was a mechanism that began so early after the incident. I do not know the conclusion. Although I tried to scan the sheet of names, the quality of the copy was such that the names were unreadable.

War is truly hell!

WASH, SHAVE AND DRINK KOBLENZ'S CHAMPAGNE

We captured Koblenz. It was a city so beautiful that even with all the wrecked crumbled buildings, one could discern its graceful beauty.

Our company's mission was to clear the downtown, business section of the enemy. There were high-rise buildings everywhere, a new experience for us. Luckily, there was not much action for our platoon. Most of the Krauts had left. However, the experience was truly memorable—in two ways!

In the basement of one of the high rises we found a cache of champagne, case after case after case of champagne. Man, we never knew so much champagne existed!

Those of us who did not get looped, or finally got tired of swigging this stuff down, got very innovative. We began using it for all of our hygienic functions. Water scarce—we were moving so fast. We savored every drop keeping our canteen tightly capped.

For our hygiene i.e. washing or shaving we used the water supply "provided" by the kitchen for breakfast—a very infrequent experience.

When the mess kit was empty of food one dumped the leftovers in a barrel, then moved to another barrel filled with hot water for the first rinse, then on to the last barrel for the final rinse. That water was our supply for washing and shaving! It was always sudsy and sort of greasy for *easier shaving, my dear!*

Our liberated champagne was a glorious, bubbly substitute for that! Typical of the American GI, always creative, taking advantage of every opportunity, we made the most of it. We drank, we shaved and we cheered everybody on with this bubbly stuff—and it was all free!

Later three of the guys, drunk out if their minds, decided to take a little personal R and R and tour this wonderful place.

The leader was a bright gentleman, Cohan, who was famous for his escapades, one of which was "earning" a Purple Heart in battle, by cutting himself when opening up a can of "C" rations. He would have been an award winning writer of fiction!

Anyway, Cohan and two of his buddies, all inebriated beyond hope, wandered through the part of the Koblenz that had been cleared. Except for one thing: it had not been cleared!

Cohan always pushed the envelope and enjoyed doing it. He decided to play a game on his buddies-in-arms. He pulled the pin from a grenade, holding it with the handle but with the safety pin removed.

Now these guys were walking through a devastated city cleared of the enemy, nevertheless still dangerous, drunk out of their minds with their "leader" carrying an armed, ready to explode grenade in his hand.

His buddies kept bugging him to put the damn pin back because, "Cohan, yagonna drop the sumbitch and we'll get killed!" He finally ceded to their wishes, but rather than replacing the pin he threw it like a baseball at a fence about 200 feet away.

At that they hit the ground and the thing went off, making one hell of a racket. Debris flew everywhere.

Turning around they sauntered back towards the company with Cohan giggling at his "joke." That was except that it wasn't! Cohan yells, "Look what's going on." Coming from the area where the grenade exploded was a white flag of surrender flapping in the wind. The grenade went off near the entrance to a basement of a tall building. Soldier after soldier emerged from underground. "General" Cohan and his "troops" had "captured" about 55 German infantrymen. Cohan, always on top of things, returned the salute of the commanding officer, a young lieutenant. He accepted his Luger, his weapon of surrender, and motioned for them to lay their weapons on the ground. Cohan then ceremoniously removed the lieutenant's wristwatch and directed them to march.

Imagine this scene. We have cleared Koblenz. We are in a safe area, yet here comes drunk-out-of-his-mind Cohan and his two staggering buddies parading 55 German infantryman in a very disciplined way yelling his commands, "Hut two, three, four, hut two, three, four." The Germans, though bewildered by these funny noises did it perfectly.

The heroes returned! Damn, they were heroes! They had captured 55 of the enemy without knowing where they were or how they did it, but it was wonderful!

Some 345th men near a welcoming sign in Koblenz.

Three infantrymen of the 87th Division warily advance towards a suspected sniper nest in Koblenz, Germany. Company E, Second battalion. 345th Regiment.

Pictures – In Plauen Germany

This is me on the left, then Dave Gluck, then Al Fahey. Al is about 30, the old guy. I am 19 and Dave is 20. Taken at an ammunition dump we were guarding after May 7, 1945 in Plauen, Germany, near the Czechoslovakian border. I had gotten my front tooth knocked out in some action. That is why I was not smiling…pride.

DEER ME! DON'T STEER US THE WRONG WAY!

The war finally ended in Europe. Our squad was assigned to protect a small ammunition dump located in the middle of a glorious, verdant, picturesque area. Deer roamed freely early in the morning and late in the afternoon in the small distance.

Being bored and having nothing to do, just a handful of men, we managed to create havoc with our environment.

First, we found a beautiful convertible Mercedes command car hidden under some straw in a barn. We drove it around and finally decided to use it as target practice. We left it full of machine gun holes, literally destroying it.

Just prior to the end of the war he had liberated a large warehouse in one of the towns we captured. Strange things were in that warehouse. There was crate after crate of—would you believe—beautiful long rayon blue women's bloomers. Man, were they sexy and slinky against your body.

We kept seeing deer walking around as if they owned the place. We decided to go deer hunting. Again, under the guidance of our supreme leader, Walter Silva, he, I, and Bruce decided to go find us a deer. We would return as heroes bringing fresh venison. Our mates would do the cooking. We would enjoy a sumptuous feast.

Man, we looked and looked. We could not find any deer anywhere. Now it was getting late, and we were about to go back to our friends who had bet that we would not succeed and admit defeat.

Then we spied our quarry. It was not a deer. It looked like a deer, but it was a small steer. We had an epiphany. Here is our victim, let's kill it, skin the hind quarters, and return with beautiful beef. It would not be venison but who could tell the difference?

The animal was in a one-acre, sloping piece of ground enclosed by a wooden fence. As we walked in, Mr. Steer gave us a baleful look and trotted away.

I don't know to this day why Walter decided to kill the animal in such a unique way. I would have shot it in the head. Walter had a carbine. Bruce and I had Garands. As we sort of chased the steer up and down the steep hilled enclosure, Walter targeted the anus as the entry point for the slug. That is one difficult target, particularly when the animal is weaving around acting as if he knew what we were doing. Finally he was sort of "captured" in a corner.

Bruce and I agreed to this strange strategy by yielding to allow Silva to place the bullets perfectly where the sun don't shine even for a steer. Bang, bang, bang, bang, bang, slugs went up that poor steer's rear end. Reaction? A bit like being bitten by a flea. He took off happily trotting around the place as if we did not exist.

Walter was incensed. "Damn, that son of a bitch acts like he ain't hurt at all. I must have put eight slugs up his butt."

The procedure repeats itself and more slugs go up its butt. Finally he falls dead…probably from lead poisoning.

Now we had to take evidence of our skill back to the boys. How do you camouflage a steer's hindquarter from that of a deer? You remove it and skin it. No one ever heard of the hide on a deer's rear being white, brown and black. So, we decided to do so. Walt brought out his special Bowie knife—that is what he called it—but wasn't making much progress. Bruce decided to show him how. He pulled the blade through the animal's rear; it slipped and jammed him in his right thigh. Blood spurted out. Bruce was bleeding profusely.

The war was over; we didn't have any tourniquets. I did, though, have a spare underwear bottom in my backpack—my blue bloomers. That was to be our tourniquet.

Now picture this: The war was over, no more people getting injured, but here we came, hobbling/carrying Bruce. His thigh was festooned with a lovely, light blue—now bloody—women's rayon bloomer. This, the first wound anyone in our squad suffered post war.

We had liberated tons of those light blue bloomers in a warehouse near Plauen, plus tons of ersatz jelly—not bad, really.

Our resourceful Dave Gluck had liberated a camera. Now, Frances Tully (Tully, to us), our squad leader—one of the best—decided we should do something to raise our morale. Our destruction of the German "jeep" had kept us occupied for a while, so Tully says, "Lets' send our folks pictures of us that will make them proud!" He then proceeds to strip and replace his dirty clothes and underwear with new bloomers. To this handsome picture he added his helmet, binoculars and helmet and his M1 Garand rifle.

So there we were: Me, Tully, Dave, Al (D)* Fahey and Barbeautty, our perpetually perfumed person (*Diarrhea).

Joe our Medic, Al and Dave.

"Macho" me with the German light machine gun we used to destroy the German command car.

Me Joe and Al – goofing around

Me and Al with my P38 and his Luger

Al, Dave and me

COPS AND ROBBERS?....NO!....GOOD GUYS AND BAD JAPS!

The war had ended, and we were ecstatic — up to a point. After our stint of guarding the ammunition dump, Lt Coates, our company commander, called us together. His comments went something like this: "Gentlemen, we are elated, we are happy. The war is over with, right?"

One of the guys in the back yells, "Yes, sir!"

Coates continues, "That is correct, <u>this</u> war is over, but our boys in the South Pacific are still fighting Japan."

There was an almost discernible "Oh, shit!" whispered, but we all stood there listening intently.

"So, gentlemen," Lt Coates continued, "We will now begin the training process to teach you guys how to fight the enemy."

A muttering went through the ranks, saying, "What the hell does he mean, fight the enemy? What the hell have we been doing for two years?" Lt. Coates knew what was going through our minds. He did not pause.

"I have received a directive from Col.Suggs that this training will begin immediately. An area has been set aside in the woods," he pointed to the left at an area typically of this German countryside of beautiful, small diameter pine trees, "and that's where this exercise will commence. Life-size replicas of Japanese soldiers will be strategically placed throughout the woods. An ingenious system has been employed so that when one approaches the enemy figure they will suddenly rise from the ground, standing straight up as if to shoot you."

Al Fahey, my fox hole buddy, standing next to me, says "Son of a bitch, Piff, what are we doing playing cops and robbers?"

Lt. Coates broke in, "Okay, cut out the muttering, stand at attention, and listen to what I am saying!" We couldn't believe this. Here, after all these months of incredible battle we were about to play games, not cops and robbers, but good guys and Jap guys.

Coats said, "When you get back to your barracks, I want all of you to get 100 rounds of (Garand) cartridges and remove the bullets. Take a bar of GI soap (which was very wax like) and make a plug for the cartridge by scraping the cartridge into it. You have then made yourself some blank cartridges."

Talk about wonderment, raised eyebrows and sighs of disgust. He responded as if he read our minds, "That's it, gentlemen, get to it. That's it."

We began the process. With some effort we struggled to get the bullet out of the cartridge, took the GI soap and made a plug and put those now blank cartridges in our ammunition belt.

The next day at about 6:00 in the morning under our squad sergeant's direction, we took of into the woods and began playing good guys and Japs. You couldn't help but giggle as you did this stupid exercise. In retrospect, we figured this was done to keep us somehow occupied. All of us were anxious to go home. We had heard about the camps designated by cigarette names, like Camp Luck y Strike, Camp Camels, etc. — ours was to be Camp Lucky Strike. We were anxious to get the hell out of this war! So what do you do with a bunch of soldiers that have been going like bats out of hell for months to all of a sudden to sit around and do nothing? The answer is to have them play good soldiers and bad soldiers.

Out we went being as sneaky as we could, going through the woods. When the Jap soldier figure would jump up we'd shoot it with our blank cartridges. It was very realistic, yet a few weeks earlier, we had done the same thing with real bullets and a real enemy.

Dutch Kulenkamp, my best friend and I were together sneaking through the woods trying to find some place to goof off and hide like some large boulders or a hollow for a while. There was no way to do this. The terrain was flat, the trees tall and thin, and there was just no way.

Suddenly we heard a loud shot and simultaneously a scream. The yell turned into cuss words. "God Damn, I shot myself in the foot. Son of a bitch, medic, medic!"

Dutch turned to me and said, "What the hell is going on, Piff?"

"Beats the hell out of me, Dutch; apparently somebody shot themselves."

"With soap?"

"I don't know," I said, "Let's go find out."

A bunch of us ran over to where the scream came from. There was Bruce –a brilliant, sharp, good-looking guy, moaning and cursing himself, "The Army and these f....damn Jap figures."

Bruce had made an error. He was one of the guys lying there hidden in the brush ready to operate the rope/pulley system making the Jap figures jump up in the air. Adjacent to him and parallel to his prone body, was his M1 Garand rifle, loaded with plugged in GI soap.

In the excitement of scaring his fellow soldiers making Jap guys jump up in the air, old Bruce pulled the lanyard/rope. At the same time, we don't know how the hell he did this, he pulled the trigger on his Garand. Unfortunately, the rifle muzzle was pointed directly at the top of Bruce's right foot. The blast of that soap made one hell of a mess on his foot. There was blood everywhere.

So here we go again, Dutch, I and one of the other guys picked poor, bleeding Bruce up, and headed towards the Medic station. The GIs we passed looked at this bloody scene with mouths open and eyes bright with fear, thinking "My god, we thought the war was over. How did this guy get shot with no bullets being around?"

So ended the saga of a GI shooting himself with GI soap! One consolation, it <u>was</u> a clean wound!

CIGARRETTES: OAK LEAVES AND TOILET TISSUE?

"Cigarettes during combat in World War II" would be a good title of a book for someone to write.

I have never been a smoker. I was in the distinct minority though for combat infantrymen during World War II.

Whenever we were lucky enough to have the kitchen come up to provide hot food, at the end of the line would be receptacles for toilet paper, toothpaste, tooth brushes, and, wonderfully, packages of brand new cigarettes.

The guys, smokers, and that was about 95% of them, would stash their cigarettes all over themselves, ready for any eventuality or use.

Towards the end of the war though, we were moving so fast that the kitchen could never catch up with us. We lived and survived on K-rations and C-rations. I often wondered whether the amazing amount of flatulence generated by eating those cold bans out of a can of C-rations would be one of the contributing factors to global warming. Man, guys were pooping everywhere. You'd eat these cold beans out of a can—I hated beans—but that's all you had. Guys were farting left and right, I guess the Germans had the same problem we did. It was a stinking situation.

I stashed a package of Philip Morris, in those days they were in a brown package, in my backpack for some reason. By then we were moving so rapidly that there was no supply of cigarettes to catch up with us. The guys had resorted to taking—this is true—bits of leaves, rolling them in any kind of paper—even letter paper—and smoking those things.

Reaching into my backpack for some toilet paper I found this pack of Philip Morris. We had stopped to rest a little, sitting on the ground. I took the package out and started hitting it on my hand to force the tobacco down to make it solid like one does which creates a very distinctive cigarette sound. That is the last I remember—sort of. I was descended upon by all the guys around me.

They literally consumed that pack of Philip Morris, smoking and nurturing them. Most of the guys would not smoke the whole cigarette; they'd put it out a portion of the way, snuff out the embers, and gingerly put it back in their uniform to be smoked another day. Old Piff (or was it Puff) was a hero for a moment.

HELMET: PROTECTION...CHOCOLATE MILK...DIARRHEA

The helmet that the infantrymen wore was literally a life saver but in many ways more than just protection from being hit by a bullet or shrapnel.

One of the guys in our platoon wore his proudly. There was a hole the size of the bullet as it went in the front and a large ragged one out the back. The bullet had entered his helmet over his left ear, scraping his skull. He was as proud of that as he was of his Purple Heart.

Our battalion commander wore his helmet quite proudly too. His had a big dent in it, right at his forehead. He and a German soldier, both came round the corner of a farm house, saw each other at the exact same time. They fired. The major scored a kill, and the German almost did the same thing. His slug bounced off the major's helmet.

Our favorite use was that of a pot. When the kitchen guys came up to give us a hot meal, usually in the mornings, we would take our mess kits, rinse them in two or three barrels of water, the last of which was clean enough to use for shaving. I dipped my helmet in that and took it to where I would shave, happily using the suds and the greasy but still hot water.

Another use involved becoming part of a team for its proper utilization as a farm implement. Now and then we would see a stray cow or two in a village. Here our good ol' boy ex farmhand friends grew up on the farm and request they do a little milking for us. The container in which the milk flowed of course was the helmet.

Sometimes we would enjoy some hot chocolate. This was made by shaving small bits of the chocolate bar rations we were given into some freshly milked milk. We'd find a fireplace or make a small fire, done usually at night away from the front lines. Both times I participated, I was rewarded with a bad case of diarrhea!

WHO IS SHOOTING AT US? THE WAR IS OVER!

The war ended for us at Plauen, Germany – a lovely city near the border of Czechoslovakia. Nearby was a resort used by Germans, a picturesque place around a lovely lake. It was surrounded by small playhouse-like structures where people same to rest, change clothes for swimming and to enjoy a bottle of Schnapps.

Our company took it over for a well deserved rest. It was a welcome change to sit there doing nothing, enjoying the scenery – it was very lovely.

The makeup of a typical American unit is not one of "homogenized" persons. There are all kinds,all backgrounds. One of my buddies – we will call him John – was in our squad. John was usually unkempt. He emerged from the scrabble pool of a farm working family in Kentucky. He marveled at the real world as he saw it, all these machines and men and material and advances which he had never experienced in his young life.

John tried to be a good soldier. He kept his Garand rifle clean, though maybe not himself too well. He was somewhat kooky. His main reason for existing was to go back home to marry his girlfriend. We knew what she looked like. He had several pictures of Mary. He would describe her figure as: "Her tits aren't very big but those nipples really poke out." John was so enamored of Mary that he carried an actual part of her with him in his wallet which he kept close to his heart. Only to his closest confidants would he show this treasured item. I was one of those persons.

One day he turned to me and said, "Piff, you are one good guy. You let me talk to you about Mary all the time. Let me show you something I got from this girl." My response, "Sure, John, go ahead, what'er you got there, buddy?"

John slowly and carefully took his wallet out of his breast pocket. He pulled out a slight plastic holder and inside resting like a jewel was a pubic hair that belonged to Mary. "Oh, I said, "that is lovely" looking at him in his eyes. He was serious! This was his treasured item! "Yep", he said. "Piff, I love this thing. I keep it next to my heart. It is part of Mary." He was right all right, it was part of Mary.

Well, as I said before he was sort of kooky. One day after indulging in too many Schnapps, World War II began again for John. Here we were ensconced happily in these beautiful play-house structures and all hell starts breaking loose. The smack of bullets hitting all around us made us all dive for the ground. We were all targets. Slowly we struggled to get to our weapons trying to see from whence the firing came. Someone yelled, "It is coming from behind that big tree up there on top of the knoll." And sure it was. You could see the body of a soldier with the rifle emerging from the side of the tree peppering the area with bullets.

The shooter reloaded and did it again. Finally the firing ceased.

Poor John, drunk out of his mind, imagined himself a candidate for the Congressional Medal of Honor against this torrent of Jerrys coming at him and he was going to wipe them out single-handed. We were the Jerrys, his old buddies.

Luckily he was not wearing his helmet. Someone managed to get behind ol'John and smacked him on the head. That temporarily put him out of misery.

Poor John. When he came to he was designated latrine digger of the division. This guy dug latrine after latrine. He dug for all the companies. He dug as we moved around. I guess, in retrospect, we should change his name from John Whatever to John Latrine. Hmm, very appropriate since he pissed so many people off!

MARKSBURG CASTLE

There were no tourist attractions for us—our division—in Europe. The 87th initiation of this war began at the start of the Battle of the Bulge.

Other "old" divisions which had entered the battle initially were delayed in returning home. This allowed some leave time for visits to Paris and other touristy places. Our early return to the States in June was that we were scheduled to be one of the first divisions to attack the Japanese mainland.

The famed 700 year old Marksburg Castle located near the junction of the Rhine and Mosel Rivers afforded us our only opportunity to view a site as "tourists."

Walt Silva, our platoon leader, led us up the heights to this magnificent edifice. Someone had two pictures remaining in a camera so I guess Silva "commandeered" them, taking one of him and one of others whose names I have forgotten.

This is a picture of Walter, a brilliant young man who saw much action from day one with our division. He eventually became a career officer with the State Department with a distinguished record serving our Nation in Africa, South America and Greece.

I suggest you "visit" Marksburg Castle via the internet. Go to : www.marksburg.de/english/frame.htm (or Google "marksburg castle") Amazingly, the site allows you to tour it with revolving images!

Marksburg Castle – virtually unchanged from Medieval Times

If you don't see any navigation bar on the left side, click here!

Marksburg Castle is the only hill castle on the Rhine that has never been destroyed. It has been lived in for over 700 years and thus represents an ever-changing and developing building complex that has been growing into its present shape over the centuries.

On the Rhine's right bank, upstream from its junction with the Mosel, a hill rises above the town of Braubach. Crowning the hill is Marksburg Castle, its unusually slender keep towering above the surrounding courts and ramparts.

Beginning with the construction of the keep in the 12th century, the castle grew into its present shape throughout succeeding centuries. In the Middle Ages, the strengthening of the castle's defences became essential and urgent by improvements made to firearms. Huge outworks date from this time, as does the conversion of a gateway in the outer wall to a strong bastion. It is mainly due to these extra defence works that the castle was never seriously attacked. In more peaceful times, it was used mainly as a state prison.

Now you can visit the most original castle in the entire valley of the Loreley. This impressive castle, home of the German Castles Association set up to preserve such ancient monuments, presents a host of fascinating artefacts that brings the Middle Ages to life.

HEY GUYS....I LAID A TURD!

In one of my memoirs, I discussed getting diarrhea when drinking home-made chocolate — made in "pristinely" clean helmets from milk just milked.

My main foxhole buddy was Al Fahey from Pottstown, Pennsylvania. Al (we think it stood for Aloysius; he would never tell us; we did not blame him) was a great soldier about 30+ years old, much older that the rest of us. Poor guy, he suffered from that runny problem all the time I knew him. It sounds funny, but boy, it really wasn't.

It was always a problem when one had to relieve one's bladder or bowels and still be ready to kill someone.

As w walked through the fields and forests of Germany, we learned how to urinate walking backwards, damn hard to do! If you stopped your colleagues would be way in front. You had to run to catch up. That was a no-no and dangerous. Now how does one have a bowel movement? That was even a tougher chore to do. You tried to wait until you could stop somewhere but as the saying goes, when you gotta go, you gotta go.

It was a real pain in the ass, no pun intended; you had to unbuckle a lot of things. You had your rifle, you backpack, your gondoliers all in the way, but that's what it was.

As we went through the chow line when we got real food, there was at the end of a supply of cigarettes and toilet paper. It came in small flattened tan "roles." I kept a large supply in the space between my helmet liner and helmet, very handy.

At the end of the war, they had gathered us at various installations — tent cities — named after cigarettes. We were at Camp Lucky Strike, the latrine at Lucky Strike was at the top of the hill, and it was dug my German prisoners.

One beautiful June morning we hear a loud voice coming from that direction not knowing whether it was in fear or in celebration. Down comes Al Fahey running s fast as he could and at the top of his voice saying, "I laid a turd, I laid a turd!" Tears came into our eyes. We were all gathered around ol' Al celebrating the fact that he had finally laid a turd.

Can you imagine having the runs for weeks on end — no pun intended — bleeding from your anus and fighting a war the same time?

THIS IS ME AT CAMP LUCKY STRIKE. ALL THE CAMPS USED
PRIOR TO OUR LEAVING, WERE NAMED AFTER CIGARETTES

MISCELLANEOUS SCENES

German soldiers – found in a camera I found at site of a destroyed home.

Koblenz

On way to Le Havre

Greek displaced persons on the way home. Taken from a truck as we headed towards Le Havre after VE Day. I just managed to yell to them in Greek.

"CAN" YOU BELIEVE THIS! FOOD FROM HOME!

We were on our way home in a luxurious ocean liner! This time not on K.P. as being on the mop-slop detail coming over!

It was a gorgeous sunny day, three days out of France. I pulled a hidden prized possession from my duffle bag. My three closest buddies, Dutch Kulankamp, Dave Gluck, and Al Fahey, and I gathered together at the stern of the ship. They had responded to my request the night before to join me about 10:00 for a surprise "going home party." Al, always sardonic, said, "Okay, Piff, what the hell is going on?"

Happy-go-lucky Dutch, this time without his signature helmet cocked to the right—all of our gear was stored somewhere—said, "Oh, leave the guy alone man, it must be something going on. Go ahead, Piff, whatta you got?"

Out from a beat-up cardboard carton tumbled eight large cans. They bore no labels. Someone had scribbled with a crayon like instrument words such as fried chicken, tee-ro-pitas*. "Damn," uttered Al, "Is that food-from home?"

So with can openers at ready, we began the job to open up these little jewels. Inside were these delicious morsels of food made by my incredible mother and sisters in Atlanta. Mom was known in our community for her innovative skills in cooking all kinds of delicious meals. My brilliant sister Evelyn had located a special company that would can home-made food to be sent to the servicemen. We never knew this, but apparently there were places all over the nation where this service was offered.

After a while, beautiful, enticing aromas wafted through the breeze to other young men sitting around reading and smoking. Immediately we were surrounded by men pleading to be included in this sumptuous feast. Alas, there was not enough. Dutch, known as a deliberate, thoughtful eater, accidentally sneezed on his yet uneaten portion to keep the hordes at bay.

The scene was reminiscent of a dog with a meaty bone being approached by another dog. There were no snarls visibly but there were snarls mentally to these interlopers.

We finished this delectable meal off. Now somewhere in the depths of the Atlantic Ocean about three hours out of France are the remnants of these beautiful homemade cans of food from Atlanta, Georgia circa 1945.

*A Greek snack food of cheese wrapped in filo and baked.

COMPANY G

1. CARLOS (my pimp friend); 2. DUTCH(best buddy survived roadblock bombardment); 3. AL (30 year old fox hole buddy, diarrhea king) 4. me, and 5. BARBUTO (Barbuty) Taken at Fort Benning, GA in the Fall of 1945.

Unit Citation
"In the Name of the President of the United States"
for the 2nd Battalion, 345th Infantry Regiment
As authorized by Executive Order 9396 (sec. I, WD Bul. 22, 1943)

The *2nd Battalion, 345th Infantry Regiment, 87th Infantry Division*, distinguished itself by its extraordinary heroism, savage aggressiveness and indomitable spirit during its advance through the Siegfried Line and capture of Olzheim, Germany. From 5 through 9 February, 1945, the *2nd Battalion* attacked violently captured Olzheim in the face of extremely difficult terrain, fanatical enemy resistance, and devastating artillery fire. In this exemplary accomplishment, the battalion advanced 11,000 yards, smashing 6,000 yards through the Siegfried Line, neutralized many pillboxes and bunkers, and captured 366 enemy prisoners. The Brilliant tactical planning, rapid capture of assigned objectives and the conspicuous gallantry of each member of the *2nd Battalion, 345th Infantry Regiment, 87th Infantry Division*, are in keeping with the highest traditions of the military service.

(General Orders 246, Headquarters 87th Infantry Division, 19 July 1945, as approved by the Commanding General, United States Army Forces, European Theater (Main).)

FINALLY A VANITY PLATE FOR COMBAT INFANTRY BADGE
FOR THE STATE OF MARYLAND

For several years I wrote to our Governor and the
Department of Transportation trying to get a CIB tag.
In November 1999, a call came in from Transportation
asking if I wanted to be the recipient of the first
CIB tag issued. Secretary Procari had seen all the
letters and felt I should be issued the first one.

Tom Walsh a Viet Nam veteran of the 101st Airborne
Division, an executive at DMV, got his choice CIB
0101.

115

SIR, YOU HAVE A BABY BOY. WHAT WILL BE HIS NAME?

"Thank you nurse. Hiz name will be Tzarles!"

"Childs, Mr. Pefinis?"

"Yes, Nurse, Tzarles, which we Greeks use for the Greek name of Constantine, like Saint Constantine whose mother built the big Church in Constantinople, St. Sophia."

I had no reason to see my birth certificate until drafted. That is when I learned that my name was "Childs," not Charles. You see, "Charles" sounds like "Childs" when said with a Greek accent! I took a pen and changed it myself really, no official help needed or desired.

I am number 129. Do not know the meaning of (15). Then my Army serial number, next MOS which means "Military Occupational Specialty," 745, which is for "Rifleman."

List No.	Name	Grade or Rank	ASN	Arm or Service	MOS
121.	O'O NEELY, WARREN	(18) Pfc	38 666 084	Inf	607
122.	OARMID, LAT F.	(8) Pfc	37 702 651	Inf	745
123.	OLLAYELL, STANLEY L.	(1) Pfc	31 424 949	Inf	604
124.	OSTER, CLARENCE T.	(2) Pfc	37 584 162	Inf	607
125.	OTELE, ANTHONY	(2) Pfc	32 705 070	Inf	607
126.	OXNDE, HAROLD R.	(5) Pfc	34 425 560	Inf	745
127.	OXNDER, JOHN L.	(3) Pfc	33 051 295	Inf	607
128.	O'NEAL, RAY J. O.	(5) Pfc	34 667 145	Inf	745
129.	OETTING, CHARLES G.	(15) Pfc	34 120 750	Inf	745
130.	OILBTE, EVERT F.	(7) Pfc	36 471 042	Inf	745
131.	OIZZIPIO, ROBERT T.	(21) Pfc	35 777 444	Inf	745
132.	OOODMAN, ROBERT J.	(2) Pfc	37 029 750	Inf	745
133.	OOODY, KENNETH F.	(2) Pfc	32 406 627	Inf	745
134.	OLAFFNEY, EARL A.	(21) Pfc	33 051 558	Inf	745
135.	OREED, GENE	(6) Pfc	35 701 304	Inf	607
136.	OREED, GUENDER A.	(1) Pfc	31 405 525	Inf	745
137.	OREENMAN, WILLARD V.	(16) Pfc	36 844 584	Inf	745
138.	OREED, LLOYD M.	(21) Pfc	33 076 470	Inf	745
139.	OOULSON, ROBERT T.	(3) Pfc	32 077 050	Inf	745
140.	OOOX, THOMAS J.	(2) Pfc	33 647 125	Inf	745
141.	ARTILLO, ALBERT B	(20) Pfc	35 822 203	Inf	405
142.	ROSE, NOEL H.	(5) Pfc	35 509 155	Inf	745
143.	ROTHWELL, WILBUR R.	(5) Pfc	35 067 952	Inf	745
144.	RUNYREN, WILLARD L.	(16) Pfc	37 502 452	Inf	745
145.	SCHEIDER, DONALD E.	(16) Pfc	36 843 772	Inf	745
146.	SCHMIDT, HERBERT E.	(5) Pfc	39 105 560	Inf	745
147.	SCHOENEMAN, JAY D.	(16) Pfc	36 845 679	Inf	607
148.	SCOTT, ROLAND J.	(5) Pfc	37 655 502	Inf	745
149.	SHIRLEY, PAUL J.	(2) Pfc	35 768 769	Inf	745
150.	SNIDER, RAYMOND O.	(2) Pfc	39 085 675	Inf	749
151.	SOLLEY, HOWARD A.	(15) Pfc	44 093 084	Inf	749

7-11-45 USS WEST POINT

Berthing Space—M-3

DECK—MAIN

Time of Mess—0930 & 1730

Mess Line—No. 4

(310)

INSTRUCTIONS

Carry Life Jackets at all times at sea.
Never touch air ports at any time.
Never throw anything overboard.
Use fresh water sparingly.
Put all trash in trash cans.
No smoking in berthing spaces.
No smoking at unauthorized times.
No flashlights or cameras.

THIS WAS GIVEN TO US ON THE USS WESTPOINT
on our way home. We left Le Havre, France. There were thousands
of us. This time I goofed off...no KP like coming over.

WHO THE HECK WAS KILROY??
THIS WILL SOLVE THE MYSTERY!!

KILROY WAS HERE!

In 1946 the American Transit Association, through its radio program, "Speak to America," sponsored a nationwide contest to find the REAL Kilroy, offering a prize of a real trolley car to the person who could prove himself to be the genuine article.

Almost 40 men stepped forward to make that claim, but only James Kilroy from Halifax, Massachusetts had evidence of his identity.

Kilroy was a 46-year old shipyard worker during the war. He worked as a checker at the Fore River Shipyard in Quincy. His job was to go around and check on the number of rivets completed. Riveters were on piecework and got paid by the rivet.

Kilroy would count a block of rivets and put a check mark in semi-waxed lumber chalk, so the rivets wouldn't be counted twice. When Kilroy went off duty, the riveters would erase the mark.

Later on, an off-shift inspector would come through and count the rivets a second time, resulting in double pay for the riveters.

One day Kilroy's boss called him into his office. The foreman was upset about all the wages being paid to riveters, and asked him to investigate. It was then that he realized what had been going on.

The tight spaces he had to crawl in to check the rivets didn't lend themselves to lugging around a paint can and brush, so Kilroy decided to stick with the waxy chalk. He continued to put his checkmark on each job he inspected, but added KILROY WAS HERE in king-sized letters next to the check, and eventually added the sketch of the chap with the long nose peering over the fence and that became part of the Kilroy message. Once he did that, the riveters stopped trying to wipe away his marks.

Ordinarily the rivets and chalk marks would have been covered up with paint. With war on, however, ships were leaving the Quincy Yard so fast that there wasn't time to paint them.

As a result, Kilroy's inspection "trademark" was seen by thousands of servicemen who boarded the troopships the yard produced. His message apparently rang a bell with the servicemen, because they picked it up and spread it all over Europe and the South Pacific. Before the war's end, "Kilroy" had been here, there, and everywhere on the long haul to Berlin and Tokyo.

To the unfortunate troops outbound in those ships, however, he was a complete mystery; all they knew for sure was that some jerk named Kilroy had "been there first." As a joke, U.S. servicemen began placing the graffiti wherever they landed, claiming it was already there when they arrived.

Kilroy became the U.S. super-GI who had always "already been" wherever GIs went. It became a challenge to place the logo in the most unlikely places imaginable (it is said to be atop Mt. Everest, the Statue of Liberty, the underside of the Arch De Triumphe, and even scrawled in the dust on the moon.)

And as the war went on, the legend grew. Underwater demolition teams routinely sneaked ashore on Japanese-held islands in the Pacific to map the terrain for the coming invasions by U.S. troops (and thus, presumably, were the first GI's there). On one occasion, however, they reported seeing enemy troops painting over the Kilroy logo! In 1945, an outhouse was built for the exclusive use of Roosevelt, Stalin, and Churchill at the Potsdam conference.

The first person inside was Stalin, who emerged and asked his aide (in Russian), "Who is Kilroy?"...

To help prove his authenticity in 1946, James Kilroy brought along officials from the shipyard and some of the riveters. He won the trolley car, which he gave it to his nine children as a Christmas gift and set it up as a playhouse in the Kilroy front yard in Halifax, Massachusetts.

So now You Know!

I can not provide an attribution. This came to me via an internet message from an old Army friend.

Charles Pefinis

TWO BEERS...IN THE PHILIPINES

I had this episode blanked out of my memory, I was done with it, no more pain; it was gone, but the mind doesn't forget, it just lays in wait until a moment when you're just breezing along, thinking of the good old times and then bam! There it is back. You can't get rid of it now; you have to live with it.

When it happened, I was 19, and it was rough, now maybe I can handle it. We landed on Luzon after a couple of months. The Philippines were hot, real hot and muggy. We got a ration of two beers per week, when they were available. Not that I was a heavy beer drinker but it was the thing then. A few of us had a deal, in the corner of a bombed out building was a small space where the cooks put an ice machine for the officer's mess. One black Steward's Mate hung out with us and he stashed our beers in the ice to keep them cold. The high point of our week was when a couple of us would meet there and drink an ice cold beer. I can see us now, taking jabs at each other, putting the cold can on our forehead and trying to talk each other out of one of his beers. This day, he was there, his name; John or Jonathan, I never knew for sure. He drove a small truck with a tank on the back out of the base to get spring water for the Officer's mess. A "good kid," friendly, from Pennsylvania I think. He wasn't in my group, but I knew him from the "beer meet."

The day was clear, hot with a light breeze, there was no rain, and the beer was great. We finally broke up and John got into the truck and off he went, at the time his leaving was hardly noticed. My mind flashes on an image of the truck going out of the gate, the sun shining off the metal fittings on the tank. That was it. He was gone and we all went back to our jobs.

Later that day I was in the tower, playing cards. The Tower crew had a game going all day and night; we usually have 4 or 5 of us there at all times, sometimes all night long too. We controlled the planes and we were in touch with the Shore Patrol Jeep too. It was then that the cook called and asked if we could raise the S P's and see if they would check on the water truck. They said that John hadn't returned. Dale was out of the game so he called the S P's and got them to take a run up to the spring. We went back to the cards.

About a half hour later, the SP called and I answered. "We found him, wrecked, send some medics, looks bad." The words came over the squawk box. Everyone dropped their cards. What did he say? "He has had an accident, he's hurt."

"How bad is it," I asked over the mike.

A new voice came over the mike, "He's dead." It was then that I felt sick. No! I said to myself, and I put the mike down and sat down in the extra chair. I remember that Dale took the mike and talked to the SP. Someone called the cooks, and sickbay. The rest of us just stared at each other, a bunch of kids, shaken, unbelieving, immobile.

A while later, I went down to the officer's mess to get the latest news. I was there when the big 6x6 truck pulled in. There, lying in the back of the muddy truck, was John, blood all over his head, neck and chest. God, it was a terrible sight. I later learned he had been shot in the neck and the truck crashed into a gully, making the heavy water tank crash forward, crushing him. That image haunted me for years, and then finally I had blanked it out of my head until recently as I was searching for memories and it rose up again. I hope now at 80 I can handle it. One thing more, no one touched John's last beer.

Richard Decker

Richard was a seaman, SP(Y)3/cl, Control tower operator in WWII.

JOHN LAMBROS AND JOHN F. KENNEDY...
SAME PT GROUP

John Lambros enlisted in the Navy as an Apprentice Seaman at the end of 1942. He was sent to Midshipman School at Columbia University for 4 months and commissioned as an Ensign in March 1943. Of 900 Midshipmen in his class, Ensign Lambros and 10 others were selected for duty aboard Patrol/Torpedo (PT) boats. They were sent to the Brooklyn Navy Yard where PT squadron 11 was being formed.

A squadron consisted of 3 groups of 4 boats. Squadron 11 was moved to the PT boat Training Base in Melville, Rhode Island. Later in 1943, the squadron's 12 boats and crew were loaded aboard a tanker and transported to Panama for 1 ½ months of experience operating in the tropics and in the open ocean. By then, John was the commander of PT #183 and ready for action. In early 1944, John's squadron was again loaded on a tanker and transported to Noumea, New Caledonia, where the squadron was unloaded and ordered to make its way north, under its own power, to set up a base of operations at Rendova Island in the Solomon Islands. Its mission was to attack and sink Japanese barges and cargo vessels making their way from Japan to resupply their troops on Guadalcanal and the other Japanese-held islands in the Solomons. The battle to dislodge the Japanese from Guadalcanal was huge. Before it was over, the Japanese Air Force had lost 100 planes.

After Allied Forces had secured the island, John put his crew ashore to hunt for 37-millimeter, nose-mounted machine guns on British Bel-Aire Cobra planes downed during the battle. The one they found was brought back and mounted on the forward deck of the PT #183 to increase its fire power. Slowly, Island by island, the US forces won their way north.

At one point, the Japanese began sending out 250 mile-an-hour biplanes loaded with 500-pound bombs as a psychological weapon. The GI's called them "Washing Machine Charlies," because of their unique noise pattern. John's squadron was ordered to support an attack on the air base at Vella Lavella Island from which the Charlies were operating. En route, PT #183 was attacked by a Japanese plane and a 50-caliber bullet tore through John's right shoulder leaving a 9-inch long "track." Knocked to the deck, John's Executive Officer strapped towels around his wound and secured John wouldn't fall off the boat as it zig-zagged at full speed in a dash to avoid further enemy air action.

Because this was a night operation, PT #183 was forced to continue its operation as an integral part of the squadron's battle plan. At dawn, 6 hours later, PT #183 was returning to base, still doing its duty, skimming the coastline of the other Japanese held islands to get shore gun batteries to fire at it to disclose their positions. PT #183 would relay gun position coordinates to Army and Navy fighter pilots who were operating in the area who could destroy the shore batteries.

Finally John's boat reached its base and he was placed in a dug out serving as a hospital ward. Since his wound went through his shoulder, it had to heal from the inside out, a slow process. Each week he was moved to a different hospital, each further south, until he finally reached New Zealand and received proper care. After recovering by the end of 1944, John was sent back to his squadron's new base on Emirau. Shortly thereafter, he was sent back to the PT base at Melville, RI as an instructor in PT Boat Operations. His last assignment involved training new recruits at the Columbia Midshipmen School.

Lt. John Lambros was awarded a well-deserved Bronze Star and Purple Heart when he was discharged from the Navy in December 1945.

The PT Boat was a fighting machine, 80' long and 20' wide, with 3 Packard Marine engines capable of producing a speed of 60 knots at full throttle. It was operated by a crew of 10 enlisted men and 2 officers. For armament, it carried 4 torpedoes, 4 depth charges, and twin 20-caliber machine guns, both port and starboard. The engines were well muffled so that they so that they ran very quietly, a key to effective night operations.

CHARLES PLUMB, NAVY PILOT, HIS PARACHUTE...FOR LIFE

Charles Plumb was a US Navy jet pilot in Vietnam. After 75 combat missions, his plane was destroyed by a surface-to-air missile. Plumb ejected and parachuted into enemy hands. He was captured and spent 6 years in a communist Vietnamese prison. He survived the ordeal and now lectures on lessons learned from that experience!

One day, when Plumb and his wife were sitting in a restaurant, a man at another table came up and said, "You're Plumb! You flew jet fighters in Vietnam from the aircraft carrier Kitty Hawk. You were shot down!"

"How in the world did you know that?" Asked Plumb.

"I packed your parachute," the man replied. Plumb gasped in surprise and gratitude. The man pumped his hand and said, "I guess it worked!"

Plumb assured him, "It sure did. If your chute hadn't worked, I wouldn't be here today."

Plumb couldn't sleep that night, thinking about that man. Plumb says, "I kept wondering what he had looked like in a Navy uniform: a white hat, a bib in the back, and bell-bottom trousers. I wonder how many times I might have seen him and not even said, 'Good morning, how are you?' or anything because, you see, I was a fighter pilot and he was just a sailor." Plumb thought of the many hours the sailor had spent at a long wooden table in the bowels of the ship, carefully weaving the shrouds and folding the silks of each chute, holding in his hands each time the fate of someone he didn't know.

Now, Plumb asks his audience, "Who's packing your parachute?" Everyone has someone who provides what they need to make it through the day. He also points out that he needed many kinds of parachutes when his plane was shot down over enemy territory — he needed his physical parachute, his mental parachute, his emotional parachute, and his spiritual parachute. He called on all these supports before reaching safety.

Sometimes in the daily challenges that life gives us, we miss what is really important. We may fail to say hello, please, or thank you, congratulate someone on something wonderful that has happened to them, give a compliment, or just do something nice for no reason. As you go through this week, this month, this year, recognize people who pack your parachutes.

I am sending you this as my way of thanking you for your part in packing my parachute, and I hope you will send it on to those who have helped you pack yours!

Sometimes, we wonder why friends keep forwarding jokes to us without writing a word. Maybe this could explain it: When you are very busy, but still want to keep in touch, guess what you do—you forward jokes. And to let you know that you are still remembered, you are still important, you are still loved, you are still cared for, guess what you get? A forwarded joke.

So my friend, next time when you get a joke, don't think that you've been sent just another forwarded joke, but that you've been thought of today as your friend on the other end of your computer wanted to send you a smile, just helping you pack your parachute.

MARLENE DIETRICH WITH THE WOUNDED APRIL 1945

Marlene Dietrich raised the spirits of the soldiers of the 44th Division when she played to them in April 1945. Dietrich also was on hand at the dock in New York City to greet the division upon its return home aboard the Queen Elizabeth.

Before the advent of the war, Marlene had achieved the status of a Hollywood starlet, a true superstar. Born in Berlin, Germany, in 1901, she took up acting in her early teens. When the Nazi Party gained political power, she left Germany, immigrated to the United States and became a citizen in 1939. Dietrich openly despised Hitler and his party. After Pearl Harbor, she participated energetically in bond drives and lent her sultry voice to the production of the anti-Nazi radio broadcasts. Her vehement denouncement of the Nazi regime and her participation in the propaganda radio broadcasts aimed at Germany earned her a death warrant. Despite this price on her head, Dietrich entertained American troops with the USO throughout North Africa and Europe, usually close to the front. She withstood much privation in order to stay with "our boys." Her grueling schedule included more than performances, often done under battle conditions at the front. Dietrich not only entertained but helped out in the field hospitals and even in the mess halls. Had the Nazis caught her, she would have been executed. Yet, she volunteered and persisted. Like Bob Hope, Marlene Dietrich is a true American hero.

Our thanks go to Matt Jolma for providing this piece. His father Paul Jolma served with the 44th Division in WWII. You may learn more about this at: www.flumecreek.com, Matt's website.

GOING INTO BATTLE ARMED WITH A TRUMPET

By John Torigoe
November 6, 2008

Bountiful, Utah – It was two weeks after D-Day, a few miles from the bloody shores of Omaha Beach. An airstrip had been carved out of the Normandy countryside, costing the lives of 28 Army engineers at the hands of the German snipers.

A lone sniper still remained in the nighttime distance.

Despite the risk, Capt. Jack Tueller felt compelled to play his trumpet.

That afternoon, his P-47 fighter group had caught up with a retreating German Panzer division. As the U.S. Thunderbolts descended on their targets, they saw French women and children on top of the tanks. After an initial fly-by, the order was given to attack anyway.

"We were told those human shields were expendable," Tueller said.

Back at the airstrip, Tueller took out his trumpet. He'd used it on many a starlit night to entertain the men of the 508th Squadron 404th Fighter Group.

"I was told, Captain, don't play tonight; your trumpet makes the most glorious sound," but I was stressed," he said. He was so troubled that he was willing to take a chance the sniper wouldn't fire.

"I thought to myself, that German sniper is as lonely and scared as I am. How can I stop him from firing? So I played German's love song, Lilly Marlene, made famous in the late 30's by Marlene Dietrich, the famous German actress. And I wailed that trumpet over those apple orchards of Normandy, and he didn't fire."

The next morning, the military police came up to Tueller and told him they had a German prisoner on the beach who kept asking, "Who played that trumpet last night?"

"I grabbed my trumpet and went down to the beach. There was a 19-year-old German, scared and lonesome. He was dressed like a French peasant to cloak his role as a sniper. And, crying, he said, "I couldn't fire because I thought of my fiancé. I thought of my mother and father," and he says, "My role is finished."

"He stuck out his hand, and I shook the hand of the enemy," Tueller said. "(But) he was no enemy, because music had soothed the savage beast."

"Boy, you have strong lips"

Tueller had learned to play the trumpet as a child growing up in Wyoming. His mother, a nurse, died at 29, and his father, a bartender and alcoholic, left the next day – leaving Jack and his brother, Bob, orphans.

They left their home in Superior to live with an aunt in nearby Evanston. She gave Jack his first trumpet, and he quickly discovered he had a musical ear.

"In 1939, I was playing in Yellowstone Park in a dance band of 22 musicians at Lake Hotel. The famous trumpet player Louis Armstrong came up to the band during intermission and said, "You sound pretty good for white cats," Tueller recalled.

He asked Armstrong what advice he would give a young trumpet player. "He said 'Always play the melody, man.

Look at them, see their age group, play their love songs, and you'll carry all the money to the bank.

Tueller enrolled at Brigham Young University, where he met his future wife and fellow trumpeter, Marjorie.

"This beautiful brown-haired gal with luscious red lips said, "Did you play the trumpet solo at the freshman assembly?" And I said, "Yes, Ma'am, I did." She said, "Boy, you have strong lips." Being a sophomore, I said, "Would you like to try me?" She nodded, and I went over and kissed her."

In 1941, as war clouds gathered, Jack enlisted in the Army and was sent to fighter school because he was an "individualist", he said.

"I wanted to fly it, fire it, navigate it, shoot the guns."

He once flew his plane though a dirigible hangar at Moffitt Field in Sunnyvale, California. The Commandant was fuming mad.

"He stood me in a brace, then he kind of smiled and says, "We don't want to quell spirit like that….but don't do it again!"

When D-Day arrived on June 6, 1944, Tueller was in the air, flying five missions.

"I witnessed the invasion from a ringside seat. We saw 2 million men, 10,000 ships. And we just shot at everything," he said. "We tried to keep those men trying to get off the landing craft at high tide, where a lot of them were drowned."

"I remember feeling pride and sadness as I saw the bodies of 4,000 killed in two hours."

Tueller credits common sense and his first flight instructor, a crop duster, with his survival that day – and the rest of the war.

"I learned to love low-level flying. I never came off enemy targets high. I'd lay it down a row of trees 400 knots, a foot off the ground, so all the flak would go over my head. They'd wonder where I'd gone."

Trumpet in the cockpit

Tueller managed to fly 140 missions without taking a single bullet hole to his airplane – the name of his infant daughter, Rosanne, painted on the side.

"Everyone wanted to fly it; they thought it led a charmed."

And on each mission, Tueller carried his trumpet in the cockpit.

"I took it in a little canvas bag attached to my parachute. I figured if I ever got shot down, it would go with me, and if I survived and got put into a prisoner of war camp, I could get an extra bar of soap from the guard."

His tour of duty ended just before his fighter group left for Belgium and the Battle of the Bulge. Three months later, his plane was shot down and destroyed. The pilot was killed.

Tueller went of to fight in the Korean and Vietnam wars, and served in the Pentagon during the Cuban Missile Crisis and the Cold War. He retired in 1966 as a Colonel, having earned the Distinguished Flying Cross, almost two dozen air metals and two Legions of Merit, the nation's highest peacetime award.

Now 89, Tueller takes care of Marjorie, his wife of 68 years, who has Altzheimer's disease.

As Veterans Day approaches, he has a word of advice to veterans: "When you become a veteran, it's my opinion that you should do everything to make people realize the wonderful life that you really have."

He still has his trumpet of 70 years and still performs at schools, family get-togethers and church functions. He has a stereo system installed in the back of his family van, where he inserts a CD of big band music and begins playing the melodies of a bygone era.

"I was an unruly child," he said. "Music tamed me…My ambition as the last action on my part as a veteran is to hit high C and fall right into the grave. What a way to go!"

ANECDOTES FROM VETERANS—ANY VETERAN FROM ANY CONFLICT OR WAR FROM ANY COUNTRY

HERE ARE TWO FROM A CLOSE FRIEND JOHN REUSCHLING

I was in Oldheim, Germany, with the 29th Division where I drove the Jeep for my commander, Colonel Cooper. I remember one cold December day, all the roads were covered with ice, as was my Jeep. We used to put some sort of cover on our windshield because the ice on it caused it to really reflect the sun, making it an easy target for the Germans. It made it hard to see, though.

Colonel Cooper was a big executive with the telephone company. We were buddies. As his driver and bodyguard, I used to tell him, "If we get in a tight place and it is my ass or your ass, you know whose ass I am going to save first, don't you?"

He said, "Well, I understand, you make everything right clear."

Anyway, we were over Alldenhover one day. We were riding through the country, which had small hills up and down, you know. He was hell on gas. "Don't waste it!" He'd yell. Gas was like Patton. Gas was blood, you know. So we are riding along and I said, "Look at this, Pearly (that's what I called him), you never seen anybody do this before." So I turned the key off and the jeep automatically went up and down these small hills, you know, just drifting and saving gas. We came around a curve, and what's there but a great big German tank. Not a Tiger, but a Panzer! It was standing there right across the road and all I had seen was that God damn orange cross! There were a bunch of Germans. One guy sitting on the tank threw his damn mess kit up in the air and took off running. Believe me, to this day, I don't know how I did it. I threw that jeep in reverse and came out of there faster than I ever went in! My damn radio operator jumped out, stepping on the Colonel's back as he was going over the side. He set off running like a sonovabitch up the hill, his Goddamn overcoat flapping and goulashes slouching in the snow and everything. I came by backing up, you know, like hell bent for election! He yelled, wanting me to stop and pick him up. I said, "I ain't got time to stop and pick you up, you jumped out of the Jeep!" So he grabs a hold of the jeep on the rods where the curtain is and I dragged him all the way up the hill because the snow was pretty deep.

When I got to the top of the hill, I saw that the Colonel had put his head down under the dash in the car. I didn't know whether he thought he was going to save himself or not by doing that. Anyway, when we got up to the top about a half of a mile, me backing up, and everything was back to normal, the radio operator got back in the jeep. "Pearly" said to him, "The next damn time you have occasion like that where you go out the back, don't use my back for a foot stool!"

He said, "Colonel, when John came around the road and I saw that tank I didn't know whether to #### or go blind so I jumped! I didn't know what I was doing. I just wanted to get the hell out of there!" That was one of the funniest things that happened to me.

"Here is another one Piff."

"We had to fly to England to look at this new type of artillery shell. They called it a proximity fuse shell. It was a different kind of artillery shell, which exploded above 15 feet from contact of anything. It automatically exploded. This allowed them to shoot down more planes and blow up more open-end trenches that the Germans were hiding in. The Colonel took us with him because they had extra room on the plane. We got to London and he went to the Cumberland Hotel and we went to the Red Cross. Well, while we were there a Buzz bomb* came over and hit the hotel, so we had to go back and get his luggage, which was still there. As we entered the building we were told that his room was on the fifth or sixth floor. The bomb had really made a mess of the place and there were some Englishmen laying there wounded on the stretchers and we asked if we could be of any help and they said, "Yeah, sure, mates, you can help carry some of the wounded out."

So when I was getting ready to carry this one guy, a Cockney, out he opened his eyes and he looked up and he said, "Hi Yank, how are you doing?"

I said, "Well, we are doing all right. You are going to be all right." I offered him a cigarette, which he accepted. "We are going to take you out of here in a little while," I said. "What happened?"

He said, "Tell you the truth, Yank, I don't rightly know. I had just woke up, got out of me bed, went to have my morning piss in the pisser. I just finished and was shaking my wicky wacky. I reached up to flush it, pulled the chain, and the whole "focking" building came down!"

Now, this was because in England, the water tank is over the toilet, pulling a hanging chain flushes it. When he pulled the chain to flush it, the place blew up at that instant! He though he was responsible for blowing it up. We convinced him he wasn't.

*Buzz bomb was the name the Brits used to describe the rocket propelled flying bombs that the Germans used the latter part of the War. There was no "controlled" target. They would just fall when the fuel ran out.

This was recorded over the phone by me, as system we will use for anyone that wants to offer a submission. We are avidly requesting any stories or anecdotes anyone has to offer. Charles G. Pefenis, Editor and Publisher, see: www.howwewonthewar.com/veterans.htm. phone and details.

Please send us those experiences of yours that are not horrific or terribly bad. We want those that are amazing, inexplicable, humorous, inspiring or religious in content.

"TANKS" FOR THE MEMORIES

SUMBITTED BY AARON ELSON OF CHI CHI PRESS:

NOTES BY THE EDITOR: Aaron is the publisher of Chi Chi Press. In responding and graciously giving me permission to publish these stories, he said, "These are not 'my' stories per se but the stories of people that told them to me." Thanks again Aaron and please convey our thanks to those persons. Charles Pefinis, Editor

CHI CHI PRESS

"A good little publishing company"

In 1987, I attended a reunion of my father's tank battalion from World War II. After listening to some of the veterans reminiscing, I returned two reunions later with a tape recorder, and began preserving some of their stories. I thought, here I am, immersed in history, and this history is slowly being lost. I also thought, what a great bunch of stories these veterans have to tell. They belong in a book. I began transcribing the tapes and putting together a series of vignettes, confident I would be able to find a publisher.

After collecting enough rejection slips to wallpaper Robert Blake's prison cell, I started Chi Chi press to publish "Tanks for the Memories." My father and mother used to call each other "Chitchy," a term of endearment drawn from the Italian word "cicciolina," or dumpling. It was a personal term, and I like to think that Chi Chi Press publishes books that touch readers in a very personal way.

I followed the 1994 publication of "Tanks for the Memories" with "They were all young kids," the story of Jim Flowers, and the battle for Hill 122. Jim Flowers died in 2002 at the age of 87. Forrest Dixon, one of the principal storytellers in Tanks for the Memories, also died recently. He, too, was 87.

Jim Flowers left parts of both of his legs on a bloody field in Normandy, and his story of courage and survival has been an inspiration to many. Forrest Dixon was the maintenance officer of my father's tank battalion. Early one morning when a pair of German tanks broke through into the service area, Dixon climbed into a tank with no engine and singlehandedly knocked out a German tank. Yet I heard him remark one time that when his son Tom brought him to a reunion and fellow veteran addressed him as "Major", Jim said he didn't know his dad had been a major. Jim Flowers' daughter Janelle once said she learned more about her father's experiences during the war from "Tanks for the Memories" than she had learned growing up. These veterans simply didn't talk about a lot of things related to the war.

I once paid $85 to a literary agent named Louise Gault to evaluate the manuscript for one of my books. I had sworn I would never pay a reading fee to an agent, but the printer I have used for all my books, Ted Weiss of Langhorne, Pa., is a nut about paper, and he had me testing so many different types of paper before sending in a camera-ready manuscript that I spent over $85 on paper, and I figured I might as well spend an equivalent amount in a last-ditch effort to land a literary agent. Ms. Gault told me I didn't have a recognizable name and I wasn't a very good storyteller, and that even if I did have a recognizable name and I found a better storyteller to present the material, it would be two years before the book would see print and my so-called "market" was limited to aging veterans, many of whom would be dead before the book came out. I thought, "I could sure use that eighty-five dollars back."

The first edition of "Tanks for the Memories" sold out in 2002, and I published an expanded second edition. This year Chi Chi Press is pleased to publish a pair of new books, "Follies of a Navy Chaplain," by Connell J. Maguire, and "Love Company," by John M. Khoury. Both of these authors have a lot more in common than the use of their middle initials in their names. Both served in combat—Maguire as a chaplain with a Marine division in Vietnam, and Khoury as a rifleman with the 100th Infantry Division in the World War II. Both have important stories to tell.

Thank you for visiting the web site of Chi Chi Press. I hope you'll stay and read some of the excerpts, and consider purchasing one or more of our titles.

MORE FROM "TANKS FOR THE MEMORIES"

THE ONLINE EDITION

CHAPTER 7
THE FRYING PAN

RUBY GOLDSTEIN

One time when we were on maneuvers in Tennessee, my tank was guarding a road—this was all simulation—and the water in our five-gallon can was awful. You couldn't drink it.

There was a farmhouse by the road, so I went and knocked on the door. A woman answered, and I asked her if she had any fresh water.

She said yes, so I went back to the tank and dumped the five gallons of water out—I wasn't going to do it in front of her house—and when I returned with the empty can, she took me to a cave in the side of a mountain. There were rocks inside, and water was coming down from somewhere in the mountain.

It was crystal-clear water. I took a drink with my canteen cup. Never in my life did I taste water that delicious.

So I filled the five-gallon can to bring back to my crew. Then the woman says, "Are you fellows hungry?"

"Well, kind of."

You know what she did? She went out, and she had some fresh-killed chickens. She took the chickens, she had them all cleaned up and ready, and we had southern fried chicken, and she made biscuits for us. We were there for quite a while.

TONY D'ARPINO

You know, I've thought of this many times, if I knew then what I know now, I'd have kept a diary with names of towns. I can remember when our company took Rheims, where they make champagne.

Now, the first tank we had, behind the driver and the assistant driver there was a cubbyhole for shells for the 75-millimeter gun, but every time you wanted to use one of them, you'd skin your knuckles trying to get them out of there, so we never used it. Instead, we would pile the extra ammunition on the turret floor. When we got to Rheims, ol' Tony got the bright idea, pink champagne. I had every one of those cubbyholes filled with pink champagne. I was drinking pink champagne for breakfast, dinner, and supper.

ED SPAHR

Corporal Ed Spahr, of Carlisle, Pa., joined the 712th as a replacement in Normandy. He was a loader, and then a gunner, in C Company.

We used to have an old frying pan hanging on the back of the tank. We never washed it in water. The exhaust fumes would blow on it.

We'd stop if we saw something. One time we caught a rabbit. The rabbits were large over there, and we had a chicken and rabbit at the same time. We were out in the field, so no one knew about us eating this wild stuff. This pan would be so dirty, and we had a bucket hanging on the back of the tank as well, in which we used to brew coffee. The bucket was so black, you'd swear it was blacker than the coffee. Every time we'd get ready to eat, we'd make coffee in this, and we would say, "Well, if the meat is contaminated, if the chicken is contaminated and the rabbit is contaminated and the water around here is contaminated, these pans can't be contaminated, because there's nothing on them but road dust and exhaust fumes," and we'd eat like kings.

We'd all joke about things like that, and somebody would make some remark like, "Well, overeating with poisonous food is better than dying with a bullet."

RUBY GOLDSTEIN

We didn't have the kitchen trucks very often, so whatever you could scrounge you scrounged. We would get these big cans, put a little hole on each side, and put a piece of wire through the holes. We built a fire, we put dirt in the bottom, made holes in the bottom, put some gasoline on it, and put a smaller can on top of it, with a little bit of water. Then we went scrounging for vegetables.

One day we hit a potato field. If you hold your lever and you gun the engine, the tank turns, one tread is stopped and you're turning. What are you digging up? Potatoes.

We'd peel the potatoes, chunk them up, and throw them in. We had cans of English style stew, and we'd throw in whatever vegetables we could find. You know something? It was the best thing you ever tasted.

TONY D'ARPINO

I can't remember who thought of the idea first, but you get an empty five-gallon can with a handle on it, something like painters use, you put gravel on the bottom, about six inches, and then you put some potatoes. Then, you put about six more inches of gravel on top, and you tie it underneath—the tank had two exhausts coming out—you tie it to that. After running all day long, the potatoes are baked. We put the gravel on it so we didn't get the smell. We used to have baked potatoes all the time.

DICK GRECA

Sergeant Richard Greca was part of a maintenance crew.

In Service Company, we'd go fishing with hand grenades. Throw 'em in the river, and fish would come up, big German trout, and we'd pick 'em up.

Then one day I was in a little rowboat and I dropped one (a grenade) off the side of it. That's the last time I did that, because I discovered that the water wasn't too deep.

One night we went up to check the tanks, and the crew heard us talking, and they got scared, and thought it was the Germans out there, so they threw a hand grenade out. Two of us got hit, but not serious.

I jumped under the tank, so I wouldn't get the shrapnel, and then the doggone tank started to move. I said, "Now what?!" I got out of there real quick.

GEORGE BUSSELL

One day Eugene Crawford said we were gonna get some eggs.

I said, "How the hell are we gonna get eggs? We can't speak French."

He said, "I know how to ask for eggs. You go up and knock on the door, and when they come to the door, you say, "Avez vous des 'erf.'"

I said, "Is that right?"

139

He said, "Sure."

That's all he knew how to say. So he walks in there, he knocks on the door, and this woman comes out, and he says, "Avez vous des 'erf?'" And she shakes her head no, and he says, "Well then, where can I get some?"

RUBY GOLDSTEIN

One day when I was in the replacement depot waiting to rejoin the battalion, we were getting hungry. It was after breakfast, and it was getting close to noontime, and who knew when the heck we were gonna get chow, or what we'd get.

So this fellow and I, we took a walk, and we got to the farmhouse, where we got some eggs. We bought them. The Germans wouldn't buy them; they'd take what they wanted. I had some francs in my pocket, and said, "Give me six eggs."

I put 'em in my field jacket, three in one pocket, three in another. We went along, went into another farmhouse, and I wanted some more eggs. The woman in the house could understand what I wanted. She went out to get the eggs, and I went to sit down—forget it! I made a mistake. I crushed the six eggs in my pockets. What a mess I had!

I got the other six eggs. I cleaned up the best I could. I cleaned my pockets. Then I said, if she had a rabbit we could buy a rabbit. So it cost me, I think it was ten francs. It was about two cents per franc, so about twenty cents, and I got a rabbit. It was a nice big fat one.

We got back to camp and said, "How the hell are we gonna kill this and cook it?" So this one kid from down south, I don't remember his name, said, "I'll show you how we do it."

He took the rabbit by the hind legs on the tree. Bam! Hit the head right on the tree, held the hind legs, put the rabbit on the ground, put his foot under the neck, and pulled his head right off. Then he took a knife and gutted it.

We got a couple of branches from a tree, and two forks, cleaned them off, dug a little pit, and started a fire. I got some salt from a guy, and we poured it all inside the rabbit to clean it out, since we didn't have any water. We poured all the salt, and we were scraping it with knives to clean it out, and everybody, their mouths getting full of saliva, was thinking, "We're gonna have something to eat."

We turned that thing, and after turning it and turning it, decided it should be about done. We broke a piece off and went to eat it.

Did you ever eat shoe leather? You started chewing, you figured, look, it's better than nothing. You spit it out—you couldn't eat it.

THE FOLLOWING WORLD WAR II
COMBAT EXPERIENCES AND OBSERVATIONS IN
THE EUROPEAN THEATER WERE SUBMITTED BY:

PFC BERYL H. HAUGHT, Jr.

"A" Company---114th Infantry, 44th Division — 7th U.S. Army

1944 Photo

2001 Photo

I AM SINCERELY HONORED TO HAVE BERYL HAUGHT JR.'S STORIES AS AN INTEGRAL PART OF THESE MEMOIRS.
CHARLES G. PEFINIS

FORWARD

The following is a two volume set of some of the short stories that I have written concerning my experiences as a combat infantryman in the "ETO" During World War Two.

I am a native of Akron, Ohio, and I was drafted in the Army in early 1943, soon after high school. I had my basic training in the 75th Division Artillery at Fort Leonard Wood in Missouri.

After Basic I was an engineering student at the School of Mines in Rolla, Missouri under the Army's ASTP Program. The program was cancelled in early 1944 and I was assigned to "A" Company of the 114th Infantry Regiment of the 44th Division.

We trained at Camp Phillips, Kansas and went overseas in September of 1944. We saw our first combat on October 18th near the small French city of Luneville in Alsace-Lorraine. We were a part of the U.S. 7th Army.

On November 22nd I was wounded in the small French village of Mittlebronn by shell fragments from a German '88 Army tank gun.

I spent time as a patient in various Army hospitals in France, including those at Luneville, Vittel and Marseille, as well as one in Oran, North Africa.

I made it back to the states in late February of 1945 and spent about six months recuperating at Percy Jones General Hospital in Battle Creek, Michigan.

After my Army discharge, I returned to Akron and attended both the University of Akron and the Akron Law school under the "GI" Bill of rights.

During this period I married my high school classmate Jean and we had two daughters. Jean also served as my one and only legal secretary for the thirty years I practiced law in Ohio. We retired here to Florida in 1981.

More or less as a hobby, I began writing war stories in 1986 and I have continued to write them to this date. My friends sometimes wonder how I can remember events that happened so many years ago, but the answer is quite simple. The happenings and events that one encounters in Infantry Combat are so traumatic that it's almost impossible to forget them even if you wanted to.

"In this one respect the front-line soldier differs from all the rest of us—you, me, and even the thousands of soldiers behind the lines in Africa—we want terribly yet only academically for the war to get over. The front-line soldier wants it to be got over by the physical process of his destroying enough Germans to end it. He is truly at war. The rest of us, no matter how hard we work, are not."

The Great Ernie Pyle
Northern Tunisia, April 22, 1943

KAMARADEN

For the life of me I can't recall just why the three of us were patrolling in that particular piece of woods in Eastern France on that November, 1944 morning, but more than likely I never knew the reason at that time either.

It was probably the same old story—each of us was just following the man in front. I'll have you know I was always known as the great follower! I learned early on that the quickest way to get yourself into big trouble was to be up front leading an infantry column. This lead in military jargon is known as "the point" and it's about the last place in the whole world you want to be if you can possibly avoid it.

Now I never did claim to be much of a soldier, but I had the uncanny ability of usually ending up back at the rear of the columns and this was especially true when going into an attack. This in and of itself was no small accomplishment since about ninety percent of the rest of the guys in the outfit were all trying to end up in the back too. I was able to con the other guys into believing I was more valuable back there in case the "Krauts" attacked from the rear.

I swear that we must have spent over half our time in combat just walking around from here to there and there to here, with apparently no one having the least idea whether we were coming or going. I think what often happened, especially at night, was that the man in front of the man back at the rear and start following him, with the result that we would spend most of the night just walking around in circles following each other. If you did get up the courage to ask the guy in front if he knew where he was, the answer was always the same: "How the hell do I know, I'm just following the guy in front of me."

In fact, during the latter part of October, we in the 44th Division received a "Letter of Commendation" from General Alexander M. Patch, the Commanding General of the U.S.7th Army, which read in part as follows:

"You drove the Germans from their remaining strong points in the 'Foret de Parroy' and by your continued and active patrolling in this forest you kept the enemy from any offensive action in this section."

The General was referring to a 24-hour "forced-march" that our battalion and others made through a large forest to the northeast of Luneville, a mid-sized city in western Alsace-Lorraine. What the General didn't know was that our battalion neither shot, saw, or even as much as heard a single German in the whole damn woods. Maybe all of them directly in front of us snuck out of the other side when they heard us coming in. We never were too quiet. Apparently some of the other infantry battalions did better than us or else the division never would have received the "commendation."

Since our side did end up winning, apparently some of the officers at least occasionally knew where we were going, but they were not about to let any of us privates in on the secret, knowing full well if we were captured the first thing we would do would be to "spill the beans." They weren't right about much, but they were sure right about that!

The old business about "If you're taken prisoner only give them your name, rank and serial number" was for troops back in the rear echelons—and I mean way back in the rear echelons.

Getting back to our patrol, the three of us were walking along rather nonchalantly through the woods, with only the occasional whine of an artillery shell going overhead to distract our attention, when we stumbled onto three German soldiers sitting beside each other on a log. They made no effort to go for their weapons, nor did we threaten them with ours. We never demanded nor did they offer to surrender; we stared at each other for a long while without a word being said by anyone.

They were battle hardened soldiers, not the young boys and old men we were often accustomed to fighting. You could tell by their general demeanor and look that they had seen a lot of action. The only thing unusual was that the one in the middle was stark naked and he was one bloody mess. If he'd been hit with one shell fragment he'd been hit with at least a hundred. There were small cuts and holes all over his body, some still bleeding. He'd probably been hit with fragments from a shell (maybe even one of their own) that had exploded high up in the trees. Had it exploded closer he no doubt would have been dead. Other than for the bleeding, he seemed okay.

The one on the right finally pointed to my canteen and then to the mouth of the wounded soldier and said, "Wasser—wasser." To the best of my memory these were the only two words exchanged between us. I handed him my canteen and he held it up to his comrade's lips and handed it back to me without taking a drink himself. I motioned for him and the other one to have some too. They must have been damn thirsty for they drank it all. They didn't have any food, so we gave them all of the K-rations we had and most of our cigarettes too. They had nothing to offer us in return and we didn't expect anything either.

You might wonder why we were so compassionate when at any time one of them could have grabbed his weapon and we would have all ended up trying to kill each other in a firefight. It's not that we were so stupid or brave, but the one advantage you have in the infantry is that you often get to see your adversaries "face-to-face" and the look in their eyes often tells you when they've had enough. You could see in the eyes of these three that they were long past that point. Maybe they could see a little bit of it in ours too and that's why they never feared us.

For just a few minutes we were just six "Kameraden" trapped by a set of circumstances beyond our control, in a place where none of us wanted to be and at a time when we didn't want to be there. At least for a little while there was "peace and tranquility" between the six of us. It's rather ironic that the infantry, which has always had to do most of the fighting, will often show more compassion for his enemy counterpart than the people in his own tank, artillery and other supporting units. There is an old saying in the infantry that, "Every person more than half a mile behind your foxhole is a son-of-a-bitch."

We left them sitting on the log and continued on with our patrol. I have no idea what happened to the three after we left. Maybe they ended up getting shot or taken prisoner or it's even possible that they went back to their own line to fight some more. We cared less—once we left they became someone else's problem.

We never told our officers about this incident. I'm quite sure that most of them would neither have approved or understood. This all happened so many years ago that I can't quite remember all of the details, but I will lay you odds that once we got started back on the patrol, "Yours Truly" was in the back again bringing up the rear.

THE PRISONERS

We were involved in a classic example of the infantry advancing under the protection of its own artillery fire.

On this particular fall day in November, 1944, we in "A" Company were crossing a wide, fairly flat valley. The Germans were dug in before us on a big high hill over on the opposite side.

Our artillery shells were hitting the hill and exploding among their dug-in positions some three or four hundred yards in front of us.

As far as you could see on either side, other GIs were advancing in long columns across the valley and toward the hill.

Although it had rained almost continuously the night before, the morning turned out bright and clear, a rarity in Alsace-Lorraine at this time of year. The ground was still wet and muddy from the previous night's rain, however.

There was a narrow, dirt country road on the left side of the hill which led down from its crest to the valley floor below.

We paused near the bottom of the hill and watched the action going on above us, almost as if we were spectators at a football game. We stood by and let the 105s do all the firing and the dirty work.

The 44th Division had four artillery battalions; the 156th, 157th, 217th and 220th. We had no idea which one was backing us—about the only real thing a man in the infantry ever knows is what he learns by the ever-flying rumors.

The Germans on the hill were well within the range of our rifles—yet no one made any effort to fire at them. It was too easy to see that they were in enough trouble without adding to their misery.

They were scurrying about in the mud on the hillside trying to evade the exploding shells.

Some of them climbed out of their holes and tried to make a dash over the top to the relative safety of the back side of the hill. Some of them made it—unfortunately, some of them did not.

Throughout history, soldiers have always been hesitant about firing their rifles, usually much to the chagrin and bewilderment of their officers. The excuse in prior wars was usually that the rifles kicked too much and hurt their shoulders. Ours didn't, yet we didn't fire our rifles any more often than they did.

I just happen to believe that there's something inherently immoral and wrong for someone to shoot and kill another human being and that deep down inside most people have always felt like this, and this "gut feeling" is the real reason why most soldiers faltered when it came to using their weapons.

The artillery is lucky in this respect. Most of the time, they can fire their cannons from such a long distance away that they never have to witness the carnage and destruction that they create.

As soon as the artillery let up, the plan was for us to rush the hill, and attack the Germans in their dug-in positions.

Thank heaven, as it turned out, it didn't become necessary. All of a sudden, the artillery stopped firing and the whole valley grew quiet. It was probably one of the artillery's forward observers who had first spotted the white flag and notified the gun crews, either by radio or telephone, that the Germans on the hill were about to surrender.

The lead German came over the crest of the hill carrying a huge white flag, about half the size of a bed sheet. It was attached to a long pole and he was frantically waving it back and forth over his head.

It turned out that he wasn't alone — there were at least a couple of hundred more of them following close behind.

Now I had seen some battered and beat-up soldiers before, but they were pale in comparison to these. There wasn't a decent looking one among them.

Apparently most of the regulars and the always present SS officers had taken off earlier so they wouldn't be captured or killed by the exploding shells and they had abandoned these people to their own fate.

Most of them were either old men or young boys with a few women and girls included. They were all filthy, wet and muddy and no two of their uniforms looked alike.

Many of them had been wounded so badly, or else they were just so weak from hunger and exhaustion, that they couldn't even keep their hands up over their heads as we ordered.

Some of the wounded were walking but others were being carried "piggy-back" by their comrades. Some had bandages over their eyes and were being led by others. Apparently they had run out of medical supplies for some and had unbandaged open wounds that were still bleeding. A lot of them were sobbing or outright crying—and it wasn't only the girls.

As they passed to our rear, they were so terrified that we might harm them that they were afraid to look at us.

Back in September when we had so anxiously landed in France, it had never occurred to us that the war could ever deteriorate to such a low level as this.

Had these people been SS or even regular German soldiers, we would have made sure that we rubbed their noses in it by "goose-stepping" past them or yelling "Heil Hitler" as we passed by.

None of us said a word to them. It didn't do anything for our ego or morale to discover we were fighting against people like this—so we ended up too embarrassed to look at them.

Under normal circumstances, we particularly liked to taunt the SS. We let the "bastards" know that it was their blind faith in their leaders and their cowardice to question orders that had gotten us all in this bloody mess in the first place.

We took it out on them every chance we got, even later on when they were in our hospitals. In the 54th Field Hospital in Luneville, France where I was in a big room with about twenty of them for about three weeks, we never let them forget that they were Nazis, regardless of how badly they were wounded, and they deserved every insult we gave them.

After the last prisoner went by, we took off up the road to see if there might be any more hiding behind the hill and if there were any of their wounded that they had been unable to carry out.

While the holes on the front side of the hill were little more than slit-trenches, those on the back were very elaborate, mostly tunnels dug way back into the hillside.

In order to relieve the tension and try to forget what we had just witnessed, we played war! Oh yes, sometimes soldiers play war right in the middle of war. "Boys will be boys," as they say. Just for fun, we started shooting our rifles and throwing hand grenades back into the tunnels. We even tried to see who was the quickest at emptying a clip from his M1. I suppose all the noise made us feel important. Our sister companies probably thought that we in A Company were in one hell of a firefight.

Suddenly, out of an opening so small they could hardly squeeze through, two little German boys, probably no more than 13 or 14 at most, crawled out of one of the holes that we'd just fired into.

At first glance, they looked more comic than threatening. Their long, flowing army overcoats were so oversized that the bottoms drug in the mud. Both were crying and both seemed about half-scared to death.

Why they had failed to surrender with all of the others is anybody's guess.

After everything had quieted down, and we were getting ready to leave, someone suddenly realized that the boys were not only a nuisance to us, but a "menace" as well.

When the word came through to move out, someone, and I can't recall if it was Captain Williams or not, told me and another guy in my squad to get rid of them.

Now there are all kinds of lousy things you have to do in combat, but out of habit and routine you go right ahead and do them—like it or not. After all, isn't that what army training and discipline are all about?

The failure to obey an order when you're up on the line is something you just don't do—period. Armies in the field simply cannot operate effectively unless each and every order, regardless of how unreasonable, is fully acknowledged and carried out.

I think both of the boys realized what was in store for them.

Prodding them with our rifles, we marched them over to the other side of the hill and out of everyone's sight. We finally stopped in the middle of a clump of trees, where we knew we couldn't be seen.

By this time the boys had quieted down and had become almost serene.

In order to keep soldiers like them from surrendering, more than likely their officers had told them that if they were ever captured they'd just be shot, so even as young as they were, it appeared that they had finally resigned themselves to what was about to happen.

Since we didn't speak each other's language, it was only with their eyes that they begged for mercy, but under the circumstances, all we could do was ignore them and look away.

151

Even though they were very young, they were still the enemy and if you placed a weapon in their hands they were still quite capable of using it — and using it very effectively.

There was absolutely no question in our minds what we had to do. After all, since we were soldiers and we'd been given a direct order, we were obligated to carry it out, weren't we?

So, we did what every "good soldier" would have done under the same or similar circumstances — we turned them loose.

BERYL H. HAUGHT JR.   1989

The Army ran the single biggest educational program in the nation's history, the Advanced Specialized Training Program (ASTP). ASTP sent more than two hundred thousand soldiers to more than two hundred colleges and universities to study chiefly science, engineering, medicine, and linguistics. They were selected for their high IQs and previous educational experience and with the promise to become officers.

Academically, ASTP was later judged to have been more rigorous than both West Point and Annapolis. ASTP held the support of the powerful and influential Secretary of War Henry Stimpson.

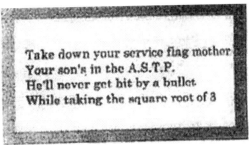

Take down your service flag mother.
Your son's in the A.S.T.P.
He'll never get hit by a bullet
While taking the square root of 3

The Army faced a crisis in 1944. They were running out of men due to heavy combat losses, especially riflemen. A partial fix, effectively shut down the ASTP and fill combat ranks will these 'whiz kids'. This freed up enough men for ten full divisions. In February 1944, George Marshall informed the Secretary of War to make a decision. If the the ASTP continued at the current level of staffing, the Army would be forced to disband ten divisions, three tank battalions and twenty-six antiaircraft battalions.

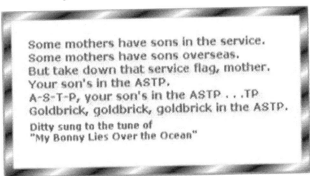

Some mothers have sons in the service.
Some mothers have sons overseas.
But take down that service flag, mother.
Your son's in the ASTP.
A-S-T-P, your son's in the ASTP . . .TP
Goldbrick, goldbrick, goldbrick in the ASTP.

Ditty sung to the tune of
"My Bonny Lies Over the Ocean"

Source: The Final Crisis Combat in Northern Alsace,
Richard Engler, page 20

"By Order of the Secretary of War," the ASTP scholar soldier students were informed that "The time has now come for the majority of you to be assigned to other active duty." That other active duty almost always proved to be in the front lines with the Army ground forces. Stimpson later predicted the outcome to them: "Your intelligence, training, and high qualities of <u>leadership</u> are expected to raise the combat efficiency of those (ground) units." Source: Louis Keefer's book "Scholars in Foxholes"

What an advantage to the Allies.   Many replacement soldiers were America's best and brightest. Author Stephen Ambrose wrote in Citizen Soldier: "What an asset- at a time when very other combatant was taking conscripts too old, too young, too ill to fight, the U.S. Army was feeding into its fighting force its best young men."

The old-line soldiers had little use for these 'whiz kids', one **was my father, a** pre-med student before the war and a graduate of the ASTP German languages school at the University of Iowa. His next assignment was as a medic with the 44th I.D., 119th Medical Battalion.

Famous ASTP soldiers include Henry Kissinger, Edward Koch, Frank Church, Roger Mudd, Heywood Hale Broun, Gore Vidal, Curt Vonnegut and Mel Brooks. The two ditties proved to be wrong. Many ASTP soldiers died, others served with great distinction in the front lines. The flag refers to an honor system employed during the war. A service flag, with a blue star for each family member in the armed forces and a gold star for the death of a service man, adorned the homes of America.

ASTP Patch

GETTING CLOSE

Beryl H. Haught, Jr.

My first introduction to at least the close proximity of the line took place late one evening when an unidentified sergeant responded to a question of our commanding officer, Captain Williams with this answer: "You dumb SOB, don't you ever ask a question like that up here again. What, do you want to get your head blown off?"

Now just what was this highly important question that our Captain had posed and that had brought on such a heated answer? He'd simply asked, "What outfit are you guys from?" Now I'd never heard a sergeant talk to an officer like that before, so it was quite apparent that we were getting ourselves into some new and different kind of ball game.

To reconstruct, after we arrived in the city of Luneville on our train trip from Normandy, it still took us almost four more days to get up to the line itself, even though it was only 20 kilometers away. In an apparent attempt to confuse the Germans of our troop movements, we tried to hide in nearby patches of woods during the day and only advance toward the front at night. Regardless of our efforts, it didn't seem to work, since "Fritz" knew exactly when and where we took over the positions and foxholes of the 314th Infantry of the 79th Division.

It was on our last night's march that the confrontation happened between Captain Williams and the Sergeant took place. Since I was one of his runners, I just happened to be close enough to overhear their whole conversation. Along with the rest of our 1st Battalion, we in "A" Co were moving up on a narrow country road when the silhouette of a half-blown down French farm house suddenly appeared out of the dark on the right side of the road.

'Home' enhancement by GIs from the 324th.

155

There were three men standing in front of the house near the edge of the road. It was too dark to make out their uniforms, so we couldn't tell if they were American MPs or not. It was toward one of these three that Captain Williams had directed his question.

Now the Captain wasn't that accustomed to being called an SOB, so he in no uncertain terms that he was a "Captain" and demanded to know the other's rank. "If it's any of your business, I'm a 'Sergeant,'" growled the GI, "And as far as I'm concerned, I don't give a damn if you're a 'General.' Nobody up here, and I mean nobody, asks such a stupid question! Where in the hell do you think you are, in Times Square?"

Captain Williams, who was clearly shocked by the outburst, simply turned and walked away. Since the line's very ill- defined, you never know exactly when you reach it, but when Sergeants chew out Captains and get away with it, you know damn well you're getting close.

When we moved out a little later on, the sergeant and the other two were standing in front of the house at the edge of the road. I can almost imagine them saying to themselves, "Give 'em a few days up here and they'll learn to keep their big mouths shut, or at least if they want to grow old, they sure as hell better!"

D BARS

If, during WW II, an opinion poll had been taken among my fellow GIs in Company A of the 114th Infantry, judging by my performance as a combat infantryman, by consensus they probably would have rated me somewhere between "an absolute misfit" and a "confirmed straggler."

Their opinion wouldn't have hurt my feelings too much since I was a draftee and never volunteered for the lousy job of rifleman in the first place.

Strangely enough, it was out of my general disdain and dislike for the whole scene (and especially my outright fear of hand grenades) that resulted in me becoming the so called "D bar king" of Company A.

Now to those of you who aren't familiar with a D bar (and to those of you who may have forgotten), it was a GI issue chocolate-type bar, with a flavor that fluctuated somewhere between "Ex-Lax" and "bitter chocolate."

It came in a package about the size of a king-size pack of cigarettes and weighed only a few ounces. Its biggest selling point was that it was supposed to be full of nourishment, including vitamins, minerals, etc. and the army said that you could subsist an entire day on just one of them as long as you drank a whole lot of water.

Actually, it was almost impossible to eat a D bar and about the best thing you could do was gnaw on it, much like a squirrel trying to get a nut out of a shell. It was impossible to take a big bite out of one—they were far too thick and hard.

Now you may question what my fear of hand grenades had to do with my becoming the "D bar king" of Company A.

I soon discovered, after only a few days up on the line, that carrying an empty pack was useless and mine was empty because I had already tossed away my shelter half, blankets, tent poles, and pegs and all the other things that were supposed to go inside. Since the damn pack straps still cut into my shoulders even though it was near-empty, the next logical step for me was to chuck it too, which of course I did without any qualms or hesitation.

The only problem remaining was the only place I had left to carry anything was in my pockets. Now C ration cans were kinda heavy and K ration boxes were very cumbersome so I had developed the habit of trading them for D bars, which fit nicely in almost any of my pockets.

I never particularly cared for the flavor of D bars but I wasn't exactly in love with the taste of the tinned cheese in K ration boxes or the taste of cold stew or hash in C ration cans either.

The officers always expected you to have at least your top front pockets full of grenades. Personally, I never trusted the things (how could I be sure the safety pin might not slip out unexpectedly?) so every time I got a chance I'd take a grenade out of my pockets, toss it in a ditch and replace it with a D bar. There was an additional benefit—D bars were a whole lot lighter to carry around. It was by this methodical process that I eventually ended up without any hand grenades and my pockets full of D bars.

I'm sure there were times when an officer saw my bulging pockets and said to himself, "Boy, now there goes a soldier who looks like he's just aching to get into a firefight."

All in all, I was always fairly sharp at math (I had even managed to eke out passing grades in both Analytical Geometry and Calculus in the ASTP program at the School of Mines and Metallurgy in Rolla, Missouri) but I could never quite get the "count" straight when it came to throwing hand grenades!

For the life of me I just couldn't remember if I was supposed to throw the grenade and count five, or count five and then throw the grenade, or count five and pull the pin and throw the grenade, or pull the pin and count five and then throw the grenade, or pull the pin, let the handle fly off, count five and then throw the grenade, or count five, hold the grenade and then throw the pin, or hold the grenade, count the pins, and then throw the handle, etc., etc.—there were just too many various combinations for me to keep it all straight.

Besides, I always felt that if I ever got close enough to a "Heinie" to throw a hand grenade at him, I'd rather toss him a D bar (sorta like a peace offering) instead of trying to hit him with a grenade. Hell, I couldn't even throw a baseball very straight—my boyhood teammates will vouch for that.

On the day I was wounded I had exactly sixteen D bars in my pockets. Now you might ask, "How in the world would you remember that?" Actually it was quite simple, since almost every morning I took an inventory count—this was one way to make sure that some of my buddies weren't snitching one or two of them from me at night while I was sleeping.

Also, when you're carrying your entire food supply as well as most of your worldly possessions around on your back, you always have a pretty good idea what you have at any one given time.

The only item I had from home was a yellow "Fuller brush" that my brother-in-law Walt gave me when I was about sixteen years old. The rest was all army issue.

It took fragments from an exploding German tank shell to end my short-lived dynasty as the "D Bar king" of Company A.

I passed out soon after I was hit so I never did have a chance to find out just what happened to all of my D bars — but I hope that the medics who came up to treat me got their "fair share."

I can't think of a bunch of guys in the whole US army who were more deserving.

THE CAST

After you're wounded, they first take you to a place called an "Aid Station." The one I was taken to happened to be in a barn along side of an old stone farm house located somewhere between the village of Mittlebronn and the city of Sarrebourg in the province of Lorraine in eastern France.

These stations are generally located a mile or so behind the line and about the only things that the medics can do there is give shots of morphine, bandage wounds and put tags on the wounded, supposedly showing the nature and extent of their injuries.

Now I didn't mind the morphine shots and the bandages, but my problems started with that damn tagging business. I'll bet it was the brain-child of some armchair general in Washington who had never been within a thousand miles of a battlefield. It seems to me that it would be much better for the doctors in the hospitals to figure out what was wrong with the wounded rather than some inexperienced medics out in the field.

Anyway, one of the medics tending to me asked if I knew where I'd been hit and I was able to tell him precisely, "My left arm is broken and I have shrapnel wounds in my right leg, my right thigh and also in my right shoulder."

He dutifully wrote it all down and added, "Your right arm is broken too!"

Now <u>that</u> made me mad. I told him, "Hey fellow! I'm the one that's wounded, not you," and I continued, "Look! I can move the fingers on my right hand and that proves my right arm isn't broken, doesn't it?" I really didn't want it to be broken and I guess that if I thought hard enough that it wasn't then it wouldn't be. Sort of the old "mind over matter" business. Nevertheless, he paid no attention to me and wrote it down on the tag. I knew my left arm was broken because I couldn't move the fingers on my left hand—even I was smart enough to know that it was broken and broken badly.

There were three or four other wounded GIs there with me and the medics told us that as soon as it grew dark they would bring up an ambulance and get us back to a hospital further behind the lines where we'd all be safe.

I remember waking up in the ambulance in the middle of the night with visions of a clean hospital room, a soft bed with clean sheets, a tile bath, warm food, pretty nurses in white uniforms, soft music and clean cut doctors.

When I did come to the following day, I found myself lying on a canvas army cot in a huge dreary room in an old abandoned school house in the town of Luneville. There were about forty wounded soldiers in the room, mostly Germans with a small smattering of French and Americans. Most were lying on the dirt floor in litters. I guess because I was an American, I at least rated a cot.

This so-called "hospital" had been a school for SS officers when Patton's tanks captured it and the army took over the building and turned into the 54th Field Hospital.

Far from what I had expected, our sheets were olive-drab GI blankets, our bathroom was bed pans, our food was cold stew and hash, the nurses turned out to be "ward boys" in combat boots, the doctors wore blood stained aprons and the music was the moaning of the wounded and dying.

Still, even this was better than lying out in that apple orchard in Mittlebonn waiting for another '88 tank shell to come in and blow me into little bits and pieces.

I was lying on the cot on my back and my left arm rested helplessly at my side. I had no feeling in it at all. My right arm was free and my hand was lying on my chest. I could raise it to scratch my nose and do some other things for myself. I sure was glad it wasn't broken too. At least I was left with one good arm that I could use.

I must have passed out again for a long stretch for when I woke up the next day I was encased in a cast over my entire body. Strangely enough they had kept my broken left arm uncovered but had encased my good right arm inside the cast, my fingers being the only things exposed. The first thing that crossed my mind was "leave it up to the good old army to screw up and put my cast on the wrong arm."

Now I knew there could have been a lot of torture devices invented throughout the centuries (remember the Inquisition?) but I think the doctor who thought up the "body cast" was by far the most sadistic of all.

I was never so uncomfortable and helpless in my entire life. I couldn't smoke a cigarette, go to the bathroom or even feed myself. I was a complete basket case.

I started screaming and yelling and one of the "ward boys," a corporal, came over to see what I wanted. I pleaded with him to cut off my cast because some doctor had made a mistake and put it on the wrong arm. I promised if he did that no one in the world could make me tell. He gasped, "What kind of a nut are you? I can't cut off your cast. If I did I would be court martialed or even worse, I'd be sent to the infantry."

I kept insisting that some young medic in the field had made a mistake when he tagged me and I showed him how I could move my fingers. I told him I had learned from my mother when I was only about six years old that your arm isn't broken if you can move your fingers. "I've never heard of such a silly thing in my life," he replied.

I told him, "Hell, every hillbilly relative of mine down in West Virginia knows that."

"What about all the X-rays and all the doctors here who've examined you?" he asked.

I answered, "I never did have much faith in X-ray machines and I never did trust army doctors—if they were any good they'd be home making a bundle of money instead of being in this stupid army." He left me lying there without another word.

Sometime during the middle of the night he snuck in the room with a saw and cut off my cast. When he finished he pulled a GI blanket up over my shoulders and left. He never told me the reason he changed his mind and I never asked.

Maybe it was because there were only a few Americans in the room and he wanted to do something special for a fellow GI or perhaps he noticed the "tell-tale blacking" of my left hand and knew I was headed for some really big trouble. I tend to believe he really wanted to get even with the army for sticking him with such a lousy job and by cutting off my cast he was in one small way getting back at them.

The following morning, when the doctor made his rounds with his usual entourage, he came up to my cot and pulled the blanket back. He stood there momentarily, white faced and speechless. He finally yelled, "Where in the hell is your cast?"

I told him, "I don't know anything. I just woke up and it was gone." I'm sure glad he didn't quiz me any further for I never did have much resistance and I'd probably squealed on the corporal the first thing.

He yelled to any aide, "Get this guy over to surgery and put another cast on him and make sure he can't get it off!" I heard him mutter as he left, "This is the damndest country I've ever seen—how in the world can a patient with two broken arms and who can't even walk manage to lose a cast in the middle of the night?"

My freedom of being out of a cast was short lived for I came to the next morning back in another one, except this time not only was my whole upper body encased but the cast even covered all of my right hand, including the fingers. I guess they were going to make sure I didn't get out of this new one some night like I had the one before.

Well, it looked like the good old army had won again. I guess they just wanted to teach me once and for all "that your arm must be broken since you can't move your fingers." Hell, that's just what I was trying to tell them all along.

It's almost unbelievable that all of this came about just because of something some medic wrote on my tag.

Incidentally, I noticed that the same time they had put me in a new cast they had also cut off my left arm. To tell you the truth, this really didn't bother me all that much since from the very moment I was hit I couldn't move the fingers on my left hand anyway.

I'm sure glad they didn't do any tagging in the operating room—they'd have probably amputated the wrong one.

This is me arriving at the Percy Jones hospital in Battle Creek, Michigan in March of 1945.

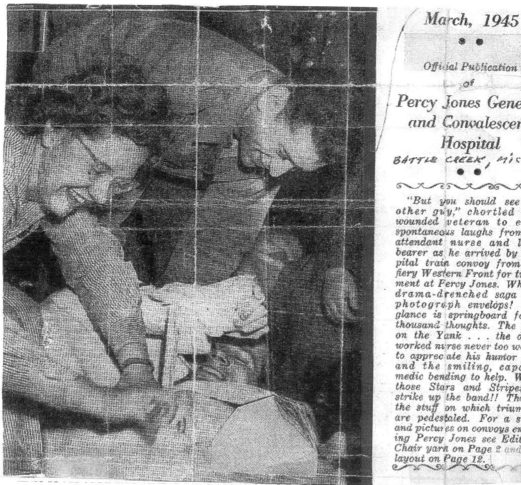

March, 1945

● ●

Official Publication
of

Percy Jones General and Convalescent Hospital

BATTLE CREEK, MICH.

● ●

"But you should see the other guy," chortled this wounded veteran to evoke spontaneous laughs from an attendant nurse and litter bearer as he arrived by hospital train convoy from the fiery Western Front for treatment at Percy Jones. What a drama-drenched saga this photograph envelops! One glance is springboard for a thousand thoughts. The grin on the Yank . . . the overworked nurse never too weary to appreciate his humor . . . and the smiling, capable medic bending to help. Wave those Stars and Stripes — strike up the band!! This is the stuff on which triumphs are pedestaled. For a story and pictures on convoys entering Percy Jones see Editor's Chair yarn on Page 2 and art layout on Page 12.

I was in honored company; three of my fellow patients later on became U.S. senators: Phillip Hart of Michigan, Daniel K. Inouye of Hawaii, and Bob Dole of Kansas

AMERICAN INGENUITY...AND SEX EDUCATION IN 'NAM!

CONTRIBUTED BY ATHAN VELLIANITIS:

One of the challenges any salesman will confront is to alter peoples' attitudes, habits and traditions. As a young U.S. Air Force officer stationed in Pleiku, Viet Nam, I was confronted with just such a situation. In this case, I was not out to sell an item to a potential customer, but to prevent hunger and perhaps starvation in a small Vietnamese village inhabited by a people ravaged by war.

As one of my additional duties, I was assigned to be my unit's civic actions project officer. This duty was a real pleasure for me since it gave me a chance to get off the air base and go into the countryside to assist the local indigenous Montagnaard tribes in improving their living conditions. All of the men who participated in the program were volunteers. My unit's expertise was in building water spillways, small dams fed by underground springs, which could give these villages a good closely available water supply.

One day the Base commander approached me and requested that I go look at a "Chieu Hoi" village, and determine if such a spillway could be constructed for them. "Chieu Hoi" literally translated meant "Open Arms." This was a program set up by the Vietnamese government for the purpose of welcoming back Communist fighters, Viet Cong, and setting them up in peaceful agrarian communities. I told the good Colonel I had never worked with the Vietnamese before but I was sure willing to give it a try.

Upon my arrival at the village with my men I surveyed the area for a damn site. We located a site with many underground springs. The village chief informed me however, that what the village really needed was food, and in particular rice. The U.S. Army Major there explained that for the first six months the Vietnamese government supported the inhabitants until they could harvest their first crops or get a small industry in operation. This village had a good concern in producing charcoal, which they would sell in Pleiku.

All was going well until one night when the Army believed it had hostile forces just outside the village perimeter. The Army fired its artillery with the shells landing short and wiping out the charcoal pit. Now there was no income to purchase the necessary food staples.

The chief asked me if I could get the village some rice. I promised him that I would do my best to do so.

I had a friend who was the director for International Development (USAID) office in Pleiku, and I approached him with my problem. He told me that because of the bad harvest he could only afford to give me a few sacks of rice but he had plenty of bulgar wheat available. I told him that he and I both knew that they would just feed the bulgar wheat to their livestock, slaughter it, and be back at square one again. He said he knew this but it was the best he could do. All of a sudden I had an idea.. I took the bulgar wheat and drove back out to the village.

The seventy or so hungry villagers gathered in their meeting hall. Through the interpreter I informed them that I acquired only a few sacks of rice but plenty of bulgar wheat. Their groans were visible if not audible. I immediately told them that I had consulted American doctors who informed me that bulgar wheat was highly recommended for increasing the size of women's breasts and increasing male sexual abilities. In a few moments the small breasted village women were in line to get their bulgar wheat while the men were waiting with big smiles on their faces.

Contributed by Athan Vellianitis, Lt Colonel, Retired U.S. Air Force, now living in Athens, Greece.

ANTHONY (TONY) LAMBROS... A REAL PATRIOT

SUBMITTED BY ANTHONY LAMBROS:

In 1989, I was part of the 45th anniversary of D-Day at Normandy. We were there to provide WWII vehicles and personnel for the gathering of veterans and families. It was an experience I shall never forget. We stayed at the Coleville-Sur-Mer, just below and east of the U.S. cemetery above the beach.

As a child I became the surrogate son of General Warfield who lived in our neighborhood. His son was killed on June 14th, '44 at Normandy. General Warfield was a kind and loving man. He died in the 1970's. One evening I walked to the cemetery to look for Teddy Roosevelt Jr.'s grave. Medal of Honor recipient graves are marked with gold leaf lettering and are easy to see, even late in the day. At that time of year in Normandy the sun does not set until 10:00 pm. The cemetery holds over 9,000 men. It is a forest of marble, gravestones which were not listed in any order, by name, date, rank, or anything that allows the visitor to find a specific individual without the help of the master directory. The building that contains the directory had long closed at 5:00 pm. I had little chance of finding Roosevelt's marker. As I strolled through the myriad isles of fallen servicemen, I felt a reverence for those lost, very hard to describe.

Suddenly, an unseen force pulled me toward a group of markers. Just as suddenly it stopped. I was in front of a grave not marked with a cross but with a Star of David. I could not explain why this happened. I was being affected by an unknown energy—extraordinary! I was alone in a graveyard.

I do not scare easily. I had no idea why the force stopped in front of a Coast Guard serviceman's cross. Unnerved I glanced around and looked at the marker behind it in the next row. It was lettered "2nd Lt. John J. Warfield Jr. June 14th, 1944, 29th Inf. Co. D, 175th."

I stood there for minutes in awe, wonder and mystery. Tears came easily. I knew then what the general had meant when he told me many years before, "Someday, you'll meet my boy and know him." As I began to leave, the nervousness left me entirely. The countless rows of white marble monuments gave me the same feeling that one has for departing old friends. It has stayed with me since.

GULF WAR...TONS OF CLOTHES...
AND PUDDING FROM HOME!!..?

SUBMITTED BY LOUIS PONTICAS:

So, prior to the launch of the ground offensive in the first Gulf War, the Marines had two light Armored Reconnaissance battalions scattered along the Kuwait/Saudi border to guard against any incursion while the buildup of the main combat force occurred behind them. I was the Platoon Sergeant of the weapons platoon in one of those companies.

My Light Armored Vehicle (LAV) was equipped with a TOW anti-tank missile launcher in a turret configuration...we had a crew of four, and we had to keep eyes on the border 24 hours per day, 7 days per week...and since my wingman and I had the only infrared night sights in the company, we had to be particularly vigilant.

Standard LAVs had a 25mm chain gun in a turret configuration and a crew of seven(which included four infantrymen). While they could split up the continuous watch across 7 Marines, we only had four, so I set up a schedule of two guys in the vehicle, eyes down-range, in four hour shifts. Of the two on watch, one could lay asleep in the driver's position while the other watched the bad guys through the turret. I had them rotate every thirty minutes to keep a turret watch from falling asleep. Once their four-hour shift was over, they could sleep or do whatever they wanted.

This was January or February while temperatures in the desert rose to seventy to eighty degrees during the day, they dropped to the thirties at night. It was not unusual to wake up with frost on your sleeping bag.

The Marines travel light. We had no winter gear, so to keep warm at night up in that turret, we put on everything we had. Personally, I would wear my tanker's coveralls as my base layer, and I'd wear my tanker's jacket on top of the coveralls. I'd wear my cammies (desert fatigues) over the jacket and coveralls. We weren't allowed to wear our tanker jacket/coveralls on the outside because everyone in the company did not have them and uniformity ruled. Finally I'd wear my thin night parka (no lining) on top of everything else. Not bad...I had gortex gloves to keep my hands warm (uh, that is until I used them once too often as oven mitts on our open fire...).

Anyway, my sister Yula sent a steady supply of pogey-bait (junk food). One day around this period she sent some Hunt's Snack Pack chocolate pudding-in-a-cup. She sent a package of six.

That night I took them into the turret for my first watch (usually around 1130 at night). I normally started my watch in the driver's seat where I could write letters. Later, I climbed into the turret and treated myself to a chocolate pudding. After my 30 minutes, I went back to the driver's slot and took me a nap. Late, when I returned to the turret, I discovered that my puddings had been smashed by either me or my gunner as we rotated jobs.

I decided the only course of action was to eat the remaining five puddings right then and there…flies would get them in the morning, and they'd go bad, and no way was I throwing them out. My gunner was already asleep, so I didn't bother waking him up.

Well, not long after eating those puddings, those puddings launched their pre-dawn assault on my digestive track. As they rapidly moved through, I realized they were intending to breach right through the other end with a speed that would preclude me from finishing my shift in the turret without a major mess on my hands…uh…in my pants, actually.

I woke up Nugent, my gunner. I ordered him into the turret immediately and after some grousing he complied.

As I jumped out of the vehicle to accommodate the rapidly advancing pudding insurgency, I grabbed the shovel, shit paper, and of course the Baby Wipes. With little water in the desert, baby wipes were as essential as bullets. We dug catholes for our bowel movements. They had to be fifty feet away from any vehicles and completely re-covered after completing your dump. Baby wipes allowed for a fresh tingling finish…just ask any baby.

Well, at zero-dark-thirty and in emergency conditions, I made it about twenty feet before I started digging in my hole. After digging and setting up (TP and baby wipes within easy reach), I rapidly dropped my pants to squat, only to remember I had all those layers on. I ripped them all off and was completely flustered when I realized I had those coveralls on. I wiggled out of those anticipating the imminent squat and download (unofficially we called #1 a Class I Download and #2 a Class II Download).

As I squatted down and prepared to fire-for-effect, I realized that all my pants and coveralls were such a mess of material at my ankles that they were more than "Danger Close" to the impact area. I gathered the clothing and swept it upward just in the nick of time.

Relieved and unscathed, I paused to reflect on the humor of it all.

Here I was, squatting with my bare cheeks in thirty degree weather over a little hole in the Saudi Arabian desert under a clear starry sky…ain't life grand?

I grabbed the baby wipes, treated myself to a fresh tingly finish, and got back to work in my little turret.

Lou Ponticas

From: Tessa Dunn
To: Pefinis, Charles
Sent: Sunday, April 22, 2007 10:30 PM
Subject: Matthew Dunn - Update – IRAQ SPRING 2007

Greetings!! We have finally heard from Matt! After more than 4 weeks of no word, he is doing okay. He sounded particularly good as he had just had his first shower in 2 weeks. It seems that they have been assigned to a Combat Outpost in a suburb of Baghdad where they stay for a couple of weeks at a time, then can go back to their FOB (Fort Operating Base) which is where they can clean up, make phone calls, and be a little more "normal." Matt is driving cargo/supply trucks—which has the danger of IEDs; they seem to be what is killing most of our American Soldiers over there, so that's kind of scary. He is also doing radio work—communications of sorts; funny—that's what my Dad did in WWII—I know he is very proud of Matthew watching him from heaven! Matt told me he was covered w/bug bites from head to toe. They sleep outside on the ground because the tents are so hot. The weather has been somewhat tolerable so far (90s), but that will change soon as 115-130 is pretty normal for there in the summer. Travis told his parents that this tour of duty is a bit better in some ways that his first in that the people who they are around (the Shiites) are more American-friendly vs. last time with the Sunnis. I got an email from Travis (not sure how he pulled that off because they aren't supposed to have email access for another month I am told); he told me that Matt was doing fine so far. We continue to be in contact with Travis' folks via email; they've been a real blessing and support; it always helps to have someone who has already "been there" at times like this. Many of you know that my computer crashed since my last email' no fun, but somehow I've managed to reconstruct most of my data, so that is why you are reading this. As always, Jim & I are grateful for all of you who continue to hold all of us up in prayer. Should you wish to send Matt or Travis a card or note, or pkg., I am sending you their addresses, as snail mail is all they have for now. Letters can go at the standard 39 cents (going up to 41 cents in mid-May), and you can get 2 sizes of FLAT RATE boxes at the Post Ofc.—both sizes mail for under $10, regardless of weight. They will give you a Customs form to fill out, the box and a mailing sticker. Take it home, fill it up, and don't pay for it until you take it ready to go. I am also sending a list of things Matt& Travis have requested:

Crystal Lite Drink flavorings (no tea flavors) or Sprots drink individually pkgd powders to add to water. No LIME flavor tho—that's all they have over there no

Hormel microwave meals

Fruit cups either individual plastic containers or cans with pop tops.

Lots of Wet Ones body wipes or baby wipes

Insect repellant

Sunscreen

Q-tips

Old Spice Deodorant & Body Wash (Matt's favorite)

Febreeze

Pistachio Nuts (Matt's favorite)

Their addresses:
PFC Matthew DUNN
A Co. 1/15 INF HQ
3rd BCT 3D
APO AE 09308

THE REAL GLENN FORD STORY

THIS ARTICLE WAS WRITTEN BY NewsMax.com
COLUMNIST AND CONTRIBUTOR PHIL BRENNAN, A PROUD MARINE.

When Glenn Ford died Thursday morning, 11-9-06, at the age of 90, major media recalled his long Hollywood career, recalling the 106 films in which he appeared, his many marriages and romances. Wrote the Associated Press, "He was a star to the end of his career."

Glenn Ford was far more than that, yet none of the obituaries bothered to mention his extraordinary patriotism or his distinguished military career. Ford rose to the rank of Captain in the United States Navy after years of dedicated service that began with World War II and continued through the Vietnam War.

He was undoubtedly a star, one of Hollywood's enduring major stars, but as his biography on a Webs site devoted to his long life states, his accomplishments were even larger than life off-screen. As his son Peter once told NewsMax.com, Gord was "one of those Ronald Regan, true-blue American types."

At the beginning of World War II Glenn served in the Coast Guard Auxiliary. In 1942 he enlisted in the United States Marine Corps. As a Marine he helped build safe houses in occupied France for those hiding from the Nazis and was among the first Americans to enter the infamous Dachau concentration camp at war's end. He went on to serve in the Navy at war's end he was commissioned a Commander in the Naval Reserves.

Committed to service in the armed forces, Ford also served two tours of duty in Vietnam with the Third Amphibious Force in 1966-1968. He once went on a jungle mission with a Special Forces Team during the Vietnam War. Ford was the only actor to have served with both the Green Berets and the French Foreign Legion and his military record is well recognized in both the United States and France as a highly decorated veteran.

Among his numerous medals and commendations are the Medal of Honor presented by the Veterans of Foreign Wars, the Medaille de la France Libre for the liberation of France; two commendation medals from the U.S. Navy; and the Vietnamese Legion of Merit. He received the rank of Captain in the U.S. Naval Reserves in 1968; retiring in 1977.

Ford bravely served his country in two wars (not on the sidelines but in the front lines) facing enemy fire on many occasions and never expecting to be treated like a Hollywood star but as a fellow fighting man. He was indeed a hero both on and off the screen.

That's the way Glenn Ford would want to be remembered.

Two years ago he told NewsMax.com, "Let's never forget that to remain free we must always be strong. That's an important lesson I learned in my Navy career in World War II. National defense must be the top priority for our country. If you are strong, you are safe. Now is the time for every American to be proud. This is the land of the free and the home of the brave. If we are not brave, we will not be free."

Glenn Ford lived the motto of the Marine Corps, Semper Fidelis. He was always faithful to the nation he served so long and so well.

Semper Fi, Glenn.

Crew of Fast Freight
722nd Squadron

Standing Left to Right:
Harry Lazot - Navigator
John R. Noblett - Bombardier
H.J. Lombard - Pilot
Randell Pillsburry - Co-Pilot
Duane P. Corporon - Flight Engineer

Kneeling Left to Right:
Carl Holland - Ball Turret Gunner
Harvey H. Rusco - Tail Gunner
Carl A. Benson - Radio Operator/Gunner
George Fulton - Right Waist Gunner

THE 450ᵀᴴ BOMB GROUP OF THE 15ᵀᴴ AIR FORCE, FLEW B-24 BOMBERS—THE FAMED "BOX CAR" IN ITALY:

NOTES FROM THE EDITOR: While creating this book, I came across this web site: www.450thbg.com. It records marvelous, sometimes poignant stories of what these heroes experienced. I took the liberty of including several of them for this book. Charles Pefinis, Editor

S/SGT HARBEY H. RUSCO

722ⁿᵈ Squadron

    S/Sgt. Harvey Rusco was a rather cheerful individual. He had brought his guitar with him and he would often sit on the edge of his bunk and play it. He seemed to have a knack for making up songs and ballads. The following gives you a pretty good idea of what was topmost on his mind. In reading it over, you could almost feel like he was reliving the routine that all of the enlisted men went through each time they went on a mission. It is very accurate and tells the story better than any of member of the crew could tell it. He was rather a small guy that just fit into the Tail Turret. He used to sing another song that has stuck in Sgt Benson's mind ever since he heard it back in 1944. It goes like this:

A GUNNER'S LIFE

A guy comes in and wakes you up'
What's coming you may dread
You're wishing it was raining
So you could stay in bed.
You go over to the Mess Hall
To get a little chow
And the coffee that they give you
Will wake you up right now.
You go back to your barracks,
Hang your mess kit on the wall;
Grab up the old flying bag
And stagger down the hall.
You go and draw a flak suit,
And lay it on your bag
All this time you're praying
Your bomb load isn't "frags."
You head then for the Briefing Room;
No one knows what's on your mind.
The reason you couldn't sleep at night
Was because of a small red line.
It could have been Ploesti'
No rougher could exist.
The boys behind those flak guns
Very seldom ever missed.
No, it's not Ploesti
Because that line of red
Isn't going in that direction;
It's going north instead.
No, it isn't Budapest;
It gets a little higher.
That line of red heads no place else
Than right straight up to Steyr.
We're briefed on several hundred guns
And fighters by the score
Your chin drops down upon your chest
As you shuffle out the door.
You get up on a G.I. truck
That takes you to your plane.
You pray to God that before too long
You can ride that truck again.

177

You check your turret in and out,
And shine the plexiglass.
To prepare for all the fighters
That are apt to make a pass.
The crew loads up, the engines roar,
With the ground crew standing by.
They pray you'll make a safe return
As they wave their fond "good-bye."
The pilot runs the engines up
We move down the taxi-ways,
And wait our turn to go;
Here the whole crew prays.
We move out on the runway;
The engines cough and whine.
The pilot moves a foot or two
To make sure we're in line.
The pilot then takes off the brakes;
We're off to see the town.
At one fifteen the stick comes back,
Now we're off the ground.
We circle the field and hour or more,
And then we're off "on course."
I clear my throat and try to talk,
But I see I'm a little hoarse.
At twelve thousand feet we all are dressed;
Now comes on the "mask."
We're set now for the job to come
It may be quite a task.
We fly for hours—we're stiff and cold.
By now our eyes are sore
From looking for the flying hell
That we've seen so much before.
Now we hear a mike switch click
And know it's going to be
"Navigator to the crew,
We're now on our 'I.P.'"
We all get set with flak suits;
The old chute close at hand.
A second look for fighters
And then a glance at land.
You pull yourself into a ball;

Your feet don't feel so bad
A cold sweat hits your face;
Your heart is running mad.
The nose gunner hits his mike switch;
His voice comes to the back,
"We must be here, boys, look ahead,
The sky is full of flak."
You wait for just a minute;
It seems an hour or more.
Then you hear that "barking" sound,
One we have heard before.
You're asking God to see you through,
For all that you really pray.
Then you hear those joyous words;
Just two, they're "Bombs Away."
The pilot rocks her sideways,
To miss a load of flak.
You're feeling pretty good now,
More sure of getting back.
About that time you see a speck,
Then a couple more.
Holy gosh, it's fighters, and
They're coming by the score.
Time to turn on turret power
And to holler to the crew.
The escort better show up soon
Or we're apt to not get through.
You're breathing hard and thinking fast;
A second more will tell.
Then you'll get them or they'll get you,
That second's really hell.
Another flock of fighters,
P-fifty-ones and thirty-eights.
They were hiding, just awaiting,
And using us as bait.
The huns peel off and try to run,
But they're a little late.
Half are meat for fifty-ones
The rest for thirty-eights.
You tell someone to pinch you
To see if you are dead

You know that mission's added
Some gray hairs to your head.
We land back at the home base;
We now feel pretty good.
We just got back on that G.I. truck
Just as we prayed we would.
Before you see your barracks
Your mind begins to roam;
And you're thinking of the letters
That you should get from home.
You realize you're back again;
How good terra firma feels.
Now you thank the Lord again,
For you're sure of three more meals.

During Word War II, I was a chaplain to the 450th Bomb Group, 720th Squadron, flying four engine Liberator bombers from near Manduria in southern Italy.

One of my assignments was gathering, inspecting and eventually mailing home the personal effects of airmen who had been shot down or were missing in action. Another was to be the morale officer, but the airmen's schedules were so crammed and rigid that is was difficult to have enough time to get to know them.

Briefing for the day's mission took place in the war room at 2:30 a.m., three, four or sometimes seven days a week. The briefings were usually very tense, with life-and-death information the daily menu. There was little time for the chaplain. Take offs were generally about 5 a.m. Formation for the mission could take an hour or more; by the time that the fliers returned to the base, they were exhausted.

The first thing that they received on their return was their "shots" to help quiet their nerves, especially if the mission had suffered great losses. After a debriefing, they had dinner, leaving my visiting time to be hit-or-miss calls in their tents between 7 and 8:30 p.m.

At the end of each mission, as the planes returned, I parked my jeep so I was facing them as they landed. All I could do was wave as they came in, but they knew I was there. Most of the planes had names or paintings -- nose art, as it was called --on them. I counted them as they landed, as a shepherd counts his returning sheep.

One afternoon, as I stood by my jeep waving, I noticed a couple of the planes circling the airfield at about 1,000 feet. That meant trouble. Suddenly a jeep raced up and the driver yelled, "The C.O. wants you in the tower."

As I stepped into the tower, the commanding officer motioned me to his side. He told me that there were wounded men on one of the planes and that the mechanism that lifted the belly turret back into the plane had been shot away. The plane had lost its hydraulic systems. "There is about five minutes of gas, and the plane will then have to belly land," I recall his saying. "The gunner in that turret cannot be saved. He is aware of the situation and wants to talk with you." The colonel then turned the microphone on and told the airmen, "Chaplain Stevens is here. I'll give him the mike." What happened next still moves me almost to tears to this day.

"Robertson" -- I do not use his real name because of his last request -- told me that he was aware he was about to die. He wanted to thank everyone

-- those in the plane with him and in the tower -- for what they tried to do to save him. "Please don't tell my parents how I died," he said. "Pray for me." I prayed with my eyes on the plane. What I said to my God, I do not know. But at the last minute I turned my mike off, and there was Robertson's voice, reciting the Lord's Prayer. As I watched that plane drop the last few feet, I heard him say: "Thy kingdom come, thy will be done." And then the plane hit the ground, and the turret disappeared in a streak of sparks.

A 1990 film, Memphis Belle, recounted a similar story. I have never seen the movie. I don't want to because, I am sorry to say, I witnessed the real event.

Each year at the reunion of the 450th Bomb Group, I speak at the memorial and worship services. Some of the men had heard me recount this story; a couple of years ago, they asked me to tell it again. When I finished, there were few dry eyes in the room. Afterward, one of the men made his way to me.

"I was in that plane," he said. "We tried and tried to get that turret up and could not. All through the years, I have suddenly remembered that event, started crying and have never been able to tell anyone why."

I understand the feeling, for it is one I share each time I am reminded of aerial combat. I collected Robertson's personal effects and sent them to his parents, along with a letter telling them that he bravely died serving his country. They never knew just how brave he really was.

Choir Practice 1944

Easter Service 1944

Story submitted by Alice and Doid Raab, Pictures submitted by David Hill

Pictures provided by: Margie Myers Mulholland and Nancy Myers Relliahan, daughters of Arthur K. Myers, 721st Squadron.

I AM AN AMERICAN.

PLEASE TAKE ME TO THE NEAREST AMERICAN OR BRITISH MISSION,
OR TO THE NEAREST RUSSIAN MILITARY AUTHORITY.

THANK YOU.

JESTEM AMERYKANIN.

PROSZE ODPROWADZIĆ MNIE DO NAJBLISZEGO POSELSTWA
AMERYKAŃSKIEGO ALBO ANGIELSKIEGO, ALBO, DO NAJBLISZEG
WLADZA ROSYJSKIEGO WOJSKA.

DZIĘKUJE SERDEC

POLAND

JÁ JSEM AMERIČAN!

PROSIM VÁS ZAVEĎTE MNE K NEJBLIŽŠÍ AMERICKÉ NEB BRITSKÉ
MISI, NEBO K NEJBLIŽŠÍMU RUSKÉMU VOJENSKEMU ÚŘADU.

DĚKUJI!

CZECHOSLOVAKIA

JA SAM AMERIKANAC.

MOLIM POVEDITE ME DO NAJBLIŽE AMERIKANSKI ILI ENGLESKE MISIJE,
ILI DO NAJBLIŽE RUSKE VOJNICKE VLASTI.

HVALA

SIGNATURE

I AM AN AMERICAN AIRMAN.
PLEASE TAKE ME TO YOUR COMMANDING OFFICER AND NOTIFY NEAREST
AMERICAN OR BRITISH MILITARY MISSION IN BELGRADE, BUCHAREST,
POLTAVA OR OTHER NEARBY PLACE. ALSO, PLEASE ARRANGE FOR TRANS-
PORTATION.

THANK YOU

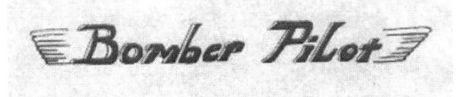

THE FOLLOWING STORIES ARE SUBMITTED BY DEWAYNE BENNETT: THE SQAWKIN" CHICKEN

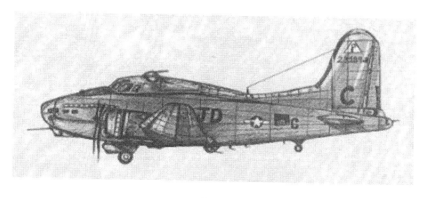

by:
Dewayne "Ben" Bennett
"The Squawkin' Chicken Skipper"
545th Squadron

(Don't miss the photo at bottom of this page!)

I was born near Lovilla, Iowa, Sept 23, 1919, and that's a fact. My Mother was 18 years old and my dad was 24. I spent the next 21 years of my life on the farm, and a great deal of that time was spent behind a team of Missouri mules. I learned a lot about them and they learned a lot about me. Mules never learned to like anybody. They would do their work with a minimum of effort, then expected to be fed and watered. They had more stamina than a horse and conserved their energy; they were smart, but would kick the bell out of you if they got a chance. They were fractious, mean and ornery, but they worked hard in the hot Iowa summer sun, pulling a turning plow acre after acre. I spent many hours alone with them.

Tom and Jerry was the last team I worked before going into the Air Force, and always attributed my success as a pilot to them mules. They were big Missouri mules, colored sort of bluish gray with white hair sprinkled through their coats. They were handsome mules, and I spent much time running a currycomb over their sleek coats. I was proud of them and liked to show them off.

In the thirties, farm boys were expected to work. School was a secondary nuisance, and not taken too serious. I got through the ninth grade of country school and was pretty proud of myself since I could read and write. I could figure how many bushels to the acre, and how much seed corn it took to plant 40 acres. That was about the extent of my formal education. We got to town only on Saturday night; that's when all the farmers went to town, sold the eggs, and bought supplies for the next week.

The women and girls would do the shopping and the men and boys would walk around the square looking for friends we hadn't seen in a week. It was a ritual, and as long as I can remember we went to town on Saturday night. It was a good place to look at girls. We didn't go to school, so our contact with farm girls was limited to Saturday nights.

I was tall, weighed about 200 pounds, and was in good shape from all the walking, lifting, pulling, and straining from farm work. We didn't have tractors, and everything was done with a team of horses or mules, and by hand. We put up barbed wire fencing, and cut our own posts from timber on the river bottom. We butchered our own meat, usually killing a hog when it got a little cold in the fall. We cut and stacked hay, planted corn in the spring and picked it in the fall, and always after dark, milked 14 cows. There was no electricity or refrigeration so the hogs we butchered had to be cut up, fried into sausage, salted down or frozen outside. We dressed in overalls, usually with no shirt, and the big brogans for foot wear. In the wintertime we wore long handled underwear, and almost every male farmer in Iowa wore a sheepskin coat bought out of the Sears and Roebuck catalog. I didn't have a white shirt or dress pants until I was 21 years old, and always felt self-conscious when I had to put them on.

We used kerosene lamps, had no radios or TV sets so reading books stimulated my imagination; took me into wonderful places and situations far away from the hard physical labor we were subjected to. I loved stories of the First World War, especially those dealing with aviation. I bought the dime pulp fiction magazines titled WAR BIRDS, SKY FIGHTERS, SKY BIRDS, and DARE DEVIL ACES and read them with a passion. I soared among the clouds engaging the evil "Baron" in mortal combat always coming out the winner. I'll never forget Robert Hogan and his Smoke Wade stories. Smoke was a sun-burned Arizona cowboy, with a ninth grade education, flying his Spad fighter and is jumped by three German Fokkers. His guns jam, and Smoke is at the mercy of his enemies.

"Angry curses sprayed through clinched white teeth. The pilot slammed back in his seat in disgust. Controls moved with lightning speed. His right hand flashed to his right leg, far down. It came up in a blur and brought with it a big, old-time Western six-gun.

"That was Smoke Wade in a tight spot. The Arizona sun-bronzed cowpoke whirled in his seat. His big six-gun spoke."

"Blam! Blam!

"The cracks came almost as fast as the answering Spandau rattle about him. One of the three remaining Fokkers leaped into the air and plunged to hell."

Old Smoke utilized every trick in the book against the Hun, but he lived to fight another day.

I devoured this pulp fiction, and looked for more. I couldn't get enough of them, but since they only came out once a month, and I devoured them sometimes in a single evening, I had to look for more reading material. That's when I discovered the public libraries in the little towns around our farm.. On our Saturday forays into town, I could usually be found in the library. All of my life I have been thankful that I discovered books and magazines at a young age. I have never been lonesome or depressed, as long as I have something to read.

In 1940 war clouds were forming, and the martial music was playing with lots of drum rolls and occasionally "Taps" was heard on the radio (by this time we had electricity). Occasionally President Roosevelt would have a "fireside chat," and we would crowd around the radio, and listen in rapt attention. That's where I first heard about the draft. I wasn't too worried about being drafted, because farming was a critical occupation and the draft board classified me as essential to the war effort. After December 7, 1941 things started to change. My draft number was 852, and I told my dad, "Don't worry, my number is so high they will never get to me."

In Washington DC, Secretary of War Stimpson put on one of those high silk hats, a frock coat, goin' to a wedding pants, and new patent leather shoes. In front of the Newsreel cameras he reached into a little fish bowl, and the first draft number he pulled out was 22. The second was 852. My draft exemption was canceled, and ten days later I was down at the courthouse for my physical. There was five farm boys like myself and the old Doctor who gave the physicals had helped in the birth of all of us. In spite of that he made us strip down, and put big red numbers on our chests. "Hell, Doc, you know all of us, why do we have to put these numbers on?"

"Cause that's the way the Army wants it," Doc said. "You fellers will all be numbers in a couple weeks anyway. You might as well get used to it."

Doc. checked us all for flat feet, and that was the extent of the physical examination. He told us to get dressed, and said we would be inducted into the service in ten days. I wanted to fly. I wanted to fulfill my dreams, and be in the cockpit of an airplane. It was time to head for Des Moines and try to enlist in the Army Air Corp.

Far from Iowa, in the very early stages of the war in Europe, the Army Air Crop. had a big decision to make. The Generals, who decided such things, were looking at heavy bomber to strategically bomb the enemy. They had ordered 340 B-18-B Douglas bombers, but Boeing had come up with the B-17 and it was ordered as the premier bomber to carry the war to the enemy.

Flying an airplane in the pre-war Army Air Corp was considered so important and difficult that only West Pointers were allowed to do it. These fellows were educated at West Point. They had to be perfect specimens. They had all their teeth, their features had to be perfect. So many hairs on their head, and the ears had to lie close to the head at an angle of not more than 10 degrees.

The pupils of their eyes must be 2 ¾ inches apart, no bags under the eyes, and the head had to be round and well formed; no pinheads were allowed. They were highly educated in English, military history, mathematics, and discipline. They were also taught the social graces, and above all taught to be gentlemen. The term "officer and a gentleman" was common in the service.

The military planners had figured out that getting a bomb on the target was going to be a difficult proposition. The pilot had to hold the plane straight and level for the bomb aimer to get the bombs on the target.

It was determined that the pilot would have to hold the plane straight and level for at least 10 minutes. In that 10 minutes every gun the enemy had would be aimed at the airplane. There would be much shot and shell, strife and bloodshed; there was no way to estimate the losses.

The truth was, there would be losses, and many of them would be pilots. Rank, education, station in life, officer and a gentleman didn't make a bit of difference. A bullet didn't recognize an officer from an enlisted man.

When word reached all of the West Point pilots there was consternation. "We're the leaders," they said to one another. "It seems foolhardy to send the leaders into such a nightmarish situation."

They were concerned, and reports flew from one office to another regarding the risk. One clerk typist, playing a joke, typed in a report "It has been estimated that ten minutes on the bomb run in a heavy bomber is equivalent to ten rounds in the boxing ring, or having your testicles squeezed for 10 seconds in a walnut cracker."

That did it, the West Pointers decided something must be done. It would be dangerous to run the risk of decimating the leadership ranks, the highly educated upper echelon officers (West Pointers), and have them fly that extremely dangerous 10 minute bomb run.

After much discussion, it was decided to have a study done by a group of high level professors. Their mission was to find out what type of American youth was dumb enough to set in that big airplane for a ten long minutes on the bomb run.

They would be like ducks in a shooting gallery, while everybody shot at them with every conceivable type of weapon intending to kill or maim them.

They engaged professors from Yale, Harvard, Princeton, Columbia, Cornell, and Penn State. The Army put them up at the Waldorf Astoria in New York, and gave them a simplified question. "Find out who's dumb enough to fly a heavy bomber on the dangerous ten minute bomb run."

The professors felt obligated to do their best. They ate big meals, and enjoyed the sights and sounds of New York while they pondered the question. They met during the day and debated the qualifications of various groups of young men. They eliminated lawyers immediately, knowing they were to highly educated to participate in a dumb thing like flying straight and level for 10 minutes while the enemy shot at you.

They argued pro and con the merits of college educated against high school educated young men. They debated for days and weeks that it took a highly educated young man to fly the mighty Flying Fortress, or the Liberator heavy bombers. After all, up to this time, only the highly educated West Pointers had been allowed to fly in the Army Air Corp.

They struggled with the question of "Who would be dumb enough to get in the cockpit of a heavy bomber, and fly straight and level for ten minutes on the bomb run?" After much sweating, straining, and soul searching, and much disagreement among themselves, they come up with a report. It had taken six months, and cost $2,000,000 dollars, but the professors felt they had given the Army Air Corp the answer they required. They were more than happy that they had found a small group of people in the United States who fit the criteria.

The only enigma in the whole report was that if this classification of folks were dumb enough to fly the bomb run, were they so dumb they couldn't be taught to fly? The professors threw up their hands on this question, they had all gained weight (eating the Waldorf Astoria cooking), they were tired and wanted to go home.

"Let the Army Air Corp figure that one out," they reasoned, as they filled out the report, signed it, and handed it to the General in charge. The professors scooted for home happy that they had done their duty for humanity and their country. The money didn't matter after all it was for their country.

Five Generals, two Colonels, three Lieutenant Colonels, one Second Lieutenant, and a private (their names are not important) were present when the report was opened. It was frill of therefore, whereas, henceforth and other related report gibberish, but it boiled down to this:

"Don't get city slickers to do this job. They are too smart to set 10 minutes in a heavy bomber, loaded with 2800 gallons of gasoline, ten 500 pound bombs, 7000 rounds of 50 caliber ammunition, with an aluminum skin that burns with searing hot flames at the drop of a kitchen match.

They will manage to evade this duty and it will all be legal which leaves the only individuals that, in our opinion, fulfill all categories of the requirement: the dumb old farm boys from the farm states.

The dumbest ones of all are those with a ninth grade education whose occupation was driving a team of mules plowing straight furrows for a cornfield. Therefore we suggest you code name your endeavor "Plowboy" and seek out at least 5000 of them for test over enemy targets".

Immediately orders went out to recruiting stations all over the United States to: "Direct your attention, and watch carefully for young men with plow boy experience, and little formal education. Commanders are ordered to survey your ranks for personnel in the above category, and hurry them into the Aviation Cadet program. The code name for this operation will hereinafter be labeled "PLOWBOY".

The "Plow Boy" program was given top priority in recruiting requirements, with the stipulation "Make it without undue speed or excitement for them to enlist, but with a confident certainty that they will enlist. Thus, the die was cast and plowboys become a valuable commodity in the recruiting wars.

With a ten-day notice to report for induction, I put on a clean shirt and headed to Des Moines. I took a bus to the federal building where the recruiting office was located, and marched right in. A Master Sergeant was behind the desk. He was writing on a piece of paper, and didn't look up. I was standing in front of the desk, and took to fidgeting, and scuffling my feet after about ten minutes of this inattention. Finally he looked up at me, and in a disgusted voice said, "Whaddya want?"

"Well sir, I'd sure like to enlist in the United States Army Air Corp, and be a pilot."

I was dressed in my overalls, a clean work shirt, and my big brogan shoes, and he looked me up and down before answering, "What the hell makes you think you're fit to be a pilot in the United States Army Air Corp? You sure don't look like much."

"Well Sir," I responded getting mildly angry, "I think I have all the smarts to be a good pilot, and I can read and write."

He looked at me in amazement, "You need two years of college or you have to pass a college equivalency test. Do you think you can do that?

I was on the defensive now, "Well, I'd sure like to try."

He sensed he was trapping me, "How much education do you have?" He was scowling as he asked me that.

"Well Sir, I finished the ninth grade."

He slapped his palm to his forehead, and in exasperation said, "You need a hell of a lot more than a ninth grade education!"

"Well sir, that's all the schoolin' Smoke Wade had."

"Who the hell was Smoke Wade?" he retorted.

"Smoke Wade was an Ace in the World War," I replied.

"I been in the Army for 20 years and never heard of him. What kind of work did you do?"

"Well Sir," I said, "I was a farmer and plowed with a team of mules. We had to plow straight furrows, and my mules were named Tom and Jerry. You might say that I was a PLOW BOY."

There was the worst clatter and banging as a chair was turned over in the office next to the recruiting office. An officer came charging through the door. He exploded at the Sergeant, "I don't want to ever hear you talk to our future pilots like that again, and if any more of these PLOW BOYS come in here I want to be notified at once!"

The Sergeant responded with a meek, "Yes sir."

Taking me by the arm, the Second Lieutenant ushered me into his office, offered me a seat, which I took, and a cigarette which I declined. He shook hands with me twice, telling me how happy he was to see me. He asked my name, straightened up his chair, and sat down facing me. He was smiling from ear to ear, as he pulled out some papers from the middle drawer of his desk. He then proceeded to tell me about the order he had just received in the mail from his superiors telling him to sign up PLOWBOYS.

"Just put your name, date of birth, and your address on this paper, and sign it," he was smiling.

I took the paper and did as he directed, and signed it. He grabbed the paper and scribbled his signature on the bottom. He told me I didn't have to take a physical, no college equivalency tests, and all I had to do was show up for the train when they shipped us to Santa Aria for our initial training.

I was feeling pretty good about being a pilot, and he reached in the middle drawer, pulled out a big rubber stamp, and slammed it down on the paper I had just signed. To this day, I DON'T KNOW WHETHER IT READ **"BP"** FOR BOMBER PILOT OR **"PB"** FOR PLOWBOY!

The old plowboy himself

"LUCKY, MASCOT OF THE 545TH"

by:

Dewayne "Ben" Bennett
"The Squawkin' Chicken Skipper"
545th Squadron

(Don't miss the photo at bottom of this page!)

He was a coal black and mangy old dog. He had one eye out (his left one I believe), one ear had been chewed off, he hopped around on three legs, and his tail had been broken. He had been castrated, and we called him "Lucky."

He was aloof, kept to himself, but attached himself to the 545th Squadron. He had been around for some time, a long time in combat years.

I have a picture of him streaking past a parade honoring the transition of Grafton Underwood from the British to the United States Army Air Corps.

This happened on July 4, 1943. The picture is shown here, and you can see the black streak at the front of the formation, blurred and hard to see, but he's there.

Over the year, he had attached himself to various members of the 545th Squadron. Most of the crews he had watched over had survived, and the beat up mangy old black dog remained loyal to the 545th. He would sleep outside the barracks by day, and at night would wander from one 545th plane to the next. He had grease all over him from being around the engine changes, but he would once in a while go into the crew chief's tent of a particular airplane and loaf while the crew worked on their plane.

He knew which planes belonged to the 545th and that was where he spent his nights. He would leave the flight line early in the morning, go to the mess hall (officers), and usually one of the cooks would give him a piece of steak or a ham sandwich. He then would go to the briefing room, and wait for the crews. He would pick a 545th crew, and would usually be at their hardstand by the time the truck arrived with the crew. When "Lucky" was at your hardstand it was considered a good omen. He would lie down near the crew chief's tent and watch the preparations for the mission, and as soon as the planes were off the ground he would make his way to the 545th barracks where he would sleep outside the barracks while the mission was underway.

Invariably he would be on the hardstand he had picked that morning as the aircraft returned and made its pass over the field before landing. He would stand by the crew chief's tent along with the mechanics, and intently watch the crew disembark. When all ten had left the plane, he showed no more interest and lay down. He didn't invite friendship, and avoided the efforts of the crew to be friendly.

On April 13, 1944, the 545th Squadron was decimated. "Lucky" had visited our hardstand that morning, and we were the only crew to return out of seven planes that had been dispatched. It was a blow to the entire 384th Bomb Group. Nine aircraft had gone down taking with them 90 crewmen and 28 of them had been killed in action. A few days later new crews started coming in as replacements. I'll never forget the reaction in "Lucky" when he saw Warren B. May, navigator on the Jack Liebert crew. His one good ear rose a little, and the broken tail started wagging. That old messed up tail was going back and forth like a bandleader's baton on a fast dance tune. "Lucky" had found someone to attach himself to, and he took to May like they had been friends forever.

May patted him on the head, and got grease on his hand. He had to be careful when he had pinks on and "Lucky" would get to close to him, and stain his pants. May and the ugly old black dog bonded and became almost inseparable. Where May went "Lucky" went. "Lucky" moved into our barracks and slept at the foot of May's bunk.

At the mess hall May would load up on food and "Lucky" started gaining weight. It was funny seeing May walking down to the mess hall and old

Lucky hopping along besides him. May was 19 years old, and old "Lucky," in dog years, was probably old enough to be his grandfather. May talked to him all the time, and I swear you could detect a smile on the old dog's face.

"Lucky" only went to the hardstand when May was due to fly on a mission. When May got up and dressed on the cold, damp English mornings, "Lucky" would watch him intently, and then hop with him to the mess hall. "Lucky" would go with him to briefing, waiting outside, and then while May drew his flight gear the old dog would go right straight to the hardstand May would be flying from.

Some of us knew this about the ugly old dog, that he had a sixth sense and could always find the right plane and hardstand. Tied up with our own fears and apprehensions we paid little attention to it.

On July 20th, 1944, the Liebert crew with Warren B. May as navigator took off for a mission to Nordhausen, Germany. Old "Lucky" watched the plane depart, then laid down outside by the crew chief's tent. He would lie there until the plane returned.

On this day, however, at about 2 o'clock in the afternoon "Lucky" started moaning deep in his chest. He got to his feet and hopped and moaned in a circle around the hardstand, and the mechanics knew immediately that their plane had probably gone down. Finally the old dog sat down on his crooked leg, put his head back, and let out a plaintive howl, and then started to the 545th barracks area. He was never seen again.

When the B-17s of the 384th returned, the Liebert crew aircraft was among them. The plane was firing red flares, and was allowed to make an emergency landing, and the ambulance rushed to the hardstand to care for the wounded. There was no one wounded, but in the bloodstained nose at the navigator's station, Warren B. May was dead, his head nearly blown away.

Today, many years later, with nothing left of the field but a broken up runway and a few handstands, the people of the little village hear things. When the mists hang low, and it's cold and damp outside, they hear faint sounds of engines being run up, and the laughter of young men. They pull the covers over their heads however, when they hear the howling of an ugly old black dog that nobody has seen.

Lucky

"THE TOILET STOOL ACE"

by:

Dewayne "Ben" Bennett
"The Squawkin' Chicken Skipper"
545th Squadron

(Don't miss the photo at bottom of this page!)

Americans are an ingenious lot. They look for ways to do things better and easier. Some might construe that Americans are lazy, but I like to think it's common sense, learned through years of hard won freedom. Freedom to think and a strong entrepreneurial streak in their makeup that wants to improve on any project that needs to be improved upon.

Give an American a nail, hammer and a piece of bailing wire, and watch out, he's liable to improve a procedure, or piece of equipment that has been in use for a thousand years.

I'm talking about a period of time before and during WWII, up to and through the 50s. Modern educational methods had not yet taken hold, and the public schools still educated young people. I ended up with a ninth grade education, came right off the farm and became a heavy bomber pilot in the US Army Air Corps (how I got in the U S. Army Air Corps is another story to be told later).

At Douglas, Az. Army Air Force Base in August of 1943, they put the Second Lieutenant's bars on my shirt collar and shoulders. I was a commissioned officer and a gentleman according to the standards of the US Army. I was also a good candidate for a POW or KIA tag after my name on some unknown list in the future.

It was inevitable that I was bound for a foreign shore to fight the enemy, Germany or Japan, and no matter how I schemed, malingered, vacillated, or just plain screwed off, my destiny was assured. I was an Old Plow Boy, and 1 was headed for Combat.

After I got my 2nd Lt.'s bars and wings, they gave me a 10 day leave, and I reported to Roswell Army Air Force Base in Roswell, New Mexico for transition into the B-17, The Flying Fortress. She was loaded with gun turrets, radios, switches and dials, and huge gasoline tanks. I could imagine when you loaded this thing with 2800 gallons of high octane gasoline, thousands of rounds of 50 caliber machine gun bullets, and five thousand pounds of high explosive bombs, and you were setting in the pilot's seat (which is where I'd be setting) your ass was in great danger.

It looked to me like a risky, dangerous business, and I asked if I could be transferred to cooking school. However, they said there was more applications from pilots than there were openings.

I finished up at Roswell, learned to fly that big Flying Fortress (I never did learn to start the engines, but that's another story), and was sent to Salt Lake City to pick up a crew. They were all extremely young men who looked at me with questioning eyes, "Can that stupid looking Plow Boy fly that big Flying Fortress?"

I did my best to look professional and to assure them that I was a competent pilot, and no longer a corn picker. To this day I wonder if I succeeded.

We boarded a troop train in Salt Lake City, and meandered down through Colorado to the little town of Dalhart, Texas. Dalhart is in the panhandle of Texas, and is flat prairie grass lands with some big ranches, little towns, and blizzards like I had never seen before. In the cowboy books I had read as a kid, the cowboys had dreaded the blue northerners, and I can understand why. There were a thousand pictures with the cowboy in the wind-driven snow with a calf draped over the saddle.

I came to dread that winter in Dalhart, the snow blowing and the howling wind. We were housed in primitive Quonset huts with a pot-bellied stove that burned wood or coal. It was tough getting up in the early morning and starting a fire, especially if the flap of your long winter underwear had accidentally unbuttoned in the restless nightmare (usually B-17s crashing in flames with the pilot still strapped in the seat) filled sleep. There was no let up in the training. The air war in Europe was heating up and the 8th Air Force had lost 60 bombers on one day in October. It was hailed as a great victory for the U.S. Army Air Forces, but the requests to transfer to cooking school went up dramatically among the future combat pilots.

We were now a combat crew. We were through with training, ready to go and fight the Hun. I can't say we were rearin' to go, but we were on our way. They issued us a new airplane, jungle packs, and sent us on our way from Kearney, Nebraska. We were to fly from Kearney to Manchester, N.H., to Goose Bay, Labrador, Iceland, Scotland, and then England. It was a sweat flying over the forbidding, wind whipped Atlantic Ocean; looking down from 20,000 feet it looked like bone chilling cold, and certain death to fall into its clutches

We were assigned to the 384th Bombardment Group, 545th Squadron, at Grafton Underwood, England. We were a new crew, the first one into this squadron in some time and no one went out of their way to welcome us. I flew a couple of missions as a co-pilot, and on our first mission as a crew, all of the old crews in our squadron were shot down. They brought in three crews with experience (10 missions or more) and three new crews to fill out the squadron. Two weeks later our squadron lost the three experienced crews, including the Squadron Commander, Captain Langlois, and I was the most experienced pilot in the Squadron with six missions.

One of the tactics used by the German fighter pilots against heavy bombers was mind-blowing and murderous. Our crews considered it unsportsmanlike and down right dirty. We had seen several B-17s go down from this dastardly maneuver and had been thinking and talking about ways to sting the Hun when he tried it on us. The German fighter would circle the formation paying particular attention to the ball turret gunners. They were hoping to find a plane with the turret inoperative, out of ammunition, or maybe with the gunner wounded and out of the turret. Finding his prey with an inoperative turret, the Hun would snake his way up under the wounded B-17, pull up sharply, hanging the fighter on the prop, and pour deadly 20mm fire into the unprotected belly. When the B-17 blew up, the fighter would fall off and dive straight down. The Germans called it "Der Unterbelly Caper".

This incensed our crew, and we scratched our heads trying to come up with a method that would protect the underbelly even though the ball turret was inoperative. We had ideas about dropping a large hook attached to a cable, and try to snare the fighter. We thought about dropping chains into the prop, but nobody would volunteer to stand on the bomb bay catwalk and drop the chains at the right time. It was difficult to get anyone to stand in the frigid cold bomb bay with the doors open, the wind and air stream shrieking and howling like a wounded banshee. Especially at 20,000 or 25,000 feet, then it was downright terrorizing with the bomb bay doors open. One crewman suggested we drop used engine oil on the fighter thereby fouling up his windshield, and if he couldn't see he couldn't fire, but how do we get the stuff on the Hun's airplane?

The latter suggestion straightened out our thinking, and we came up with the jellied gasoline idea. It was known at that time that oil-drilling mud (Bentonite) would gel gasoline. Could we rig up a five-gallon can of jellied gasoline, hinged in the bomb bay with a bailing wire running into the cockpit so the pilot could dump the can on command? The ball turret gunner could fire into the gob of jellied gasoline with 50-caliber tracer ammunition, and it would burn the fighter just before he started shooting. It was a bodacious idea; it was doable and we were setting around congratulating ourselves for a great idea.

Our first test came on a mission to Berlin, May 7, 1944. The weather was marginal, but we got through to the target and dropped our bombs. The five-gallon can rested in the bomb bay undisturbed, but not for long. Several Me-109s came sniffing around the formation so we told the ball turret gunner to track the fighters but not to fire. Sure enough one of the fighters started ducking in and out to see if the ball turret gunner was going to shoot at him. We held off until suddenly he was below us pulling up to hang on his prop.

When the gunner yelled "Now!", I pulled the wire and the jellied gasoline went out. In one big gob. The slipstream tore the gob apart, but some of it hit the fighter's windshield, and he was startled by the mass coming at him. He fell into a dive without firing.

We were disappointed by our lack of success, but not discouraged. We increased the Bentonite on the next try, and put in a quart of sorghum that my Grandmother had sent me. The results out of a five-gallon can were again unsuccessful, and we came back from Saarbrucken; Germany on May 11, 1944, a mighty unhappy crew. We had managed to set this gob on fire, but it was so scattered that it did no harm to the fighter. It scared the hell out of the pilot of the fighter; he thought the B-17 had exploded and was coming down on him.

Now then, here's where American ingenuity comes into the picture. This is what I was talking about at the beginning of this article. A young man, hardly 20 years old, and one of the waist gunners, (we'll call him Verlin), came to me, and said he had an idea about dropping the gobs of jellied gasoline. He told me he was hesitant to make the suggestion for fear the rest of the crew would laugh at him.

"I think I've figured out a way to drop that jellied gasoline in one big gob," be said, "but I'm afraid everyone in the crew will laugh."

"Well, what the hell, if it's a good idea we'll try it. We sure need to improve on that five-gallon can," I replied.

"Well, I got the idea setting on the crapper," he hesitated.

"Go on," I urged.

"When I flushed the stool I noticed that the water rushed out of the tank into the bowl, and it swirled and fell out of the bowl in a mass. If we could rig up a toilet stool in the bomb bay, close to the bottom of the plane, it would fall in a gob. In addition, if we could drop it slightly before the fighter pulled up the gob would travel with the speed of our plane, and fall in a curve. Don't you see, Sir, it would be just like a bomb falling out of the bomb bay only our target would be closer." He was animated and his face was flushed with excitement. "If our mixture was just right the gob would spread like a blanket, and engulf the whole fighter plane."

I was excited, as dumb as it sounded, the logic behind the idea had merit. It warranted a trial run. I told him to get the rest of the crew and start hunting up a toilet stool and tank. My actual orders to him were, "Find a stool, and I won't ask any questions."

I went to work with a five-gallon can mixing the gasoline and the Bentonite, until the mixture was right, and then added another quart of my Grandma's sorghum. We put the sorghum in the mixture to make it sticky, and by the time I had stirred all that sorghum in our mixture was fluid but sticky. We thought about mixing in a quart of peanut butter, but that would have made it so thick and sticky it wouldn't flush. We made copious notes of our mixture so we could duplicate it.

By this time the crew had returned with a toilet stool complete with a tank. They had thoughtfully covered it with a canvas tarp. I really wasn't anxious to have the crew chiefs know what we were doing to their airplane. I certainly didn't want the other crews knowing and damn sure didn't want the commanding officer to know. He probably would have taken a dim view of our idea. While we were mounting the toilet in the bomb bay my crew started calling me Captain Sticky; that name stuck to me for some time.

After we had the toilet mounted, and the bailing wire was threaded to the cockpit, we notified the crew chief what we had done, and asked him to keep quiet about it. Because I was the senior pilot in the squadron, he said it was OK, and was anxious to know how it worked. After a while he started calling me Captain Sticky.

The big day for the test came on May 13, 1944; on a mission to Stettin, Germany. Stettin was north of Berlin, and was a long drawn out mission with hours spent over enemy territory. We were now going over the North Sea, across Denmark then down to Stettin. The line on the map showed us going straight across Germany, right through the fighters and the flak. With that much time, probably about 8 hours, spent over enemy territory we were bound to run into fighters, and we were ready. There was five gallons of jellied gasoline, buttressed with a quart of my Grandma's sorghum, in the toilet tank, with the lid tied down so it wouldn't flop off in evasive action. The bailing wire was rigged from the flush valve to the cockpit on the pilot's side. We even tied a red rag to the wire loop in the cockpit so the pilot could find it in a hurry. We were ready. It was a go.

Our Group put up 18 airplanes, and the take off and forming into Group formation was uneventful. We got into Wing formation and struck out across France in pretty tight formation. As the mission progressed and the pilots got tired the formation tended to scatter or open up, and our position, number 5 in the low squadron of the low group, put us the lowest B-17 on the left side of the 56-ship Combat Wing. We were in an ideal position to test our theory, and the ammunition was ready and waiting.

Over Denmark we saw the first unfriendly fighters. They flew past us, circled ahead and made a half-hearted pass from head on. They disappeared behind us, probably to attack another wing, but five fighters continued to trail us looking for an opening to shoot somebody down. We had pulled our formation together, and they finally left us.

After dropping the bombs and turning north for our return we again became complacent. It was a beautiful sunny day, there was a lower overcast, and we were flying above the clouds; no fighters; and no flak. Everyone tended to relax, if relaxing is possible in a combat situation 500 miles into enemy territory.

The unexpected happened when two Me-109s came up through the clouds, and in a climbing position shot down two B-17s in our group. Lt. Thomas R Frances in plane 42-97404 SU-L (544th Squadron) with one crewman killed in action, and nine prisoners of-war. Lt. Charles W. Baker was the pilot in the second B-17, 43-102548 with 3 killed in action and 7 prisoners.

B-17 43-97414 Crew:

Pilot: 2nd Lt. Thomas R Francis – KIA
Co-Pilot: 2nd Lt. Maurice S. Mahoney – POW
Navigator: First Officer Herbert (NMI) Polansky – POW
Bombardier: 2nd Lt. Raymond E. Bowkley – POW
Top Turrett: S/Sgt. A. F. Brannigan – POW
Radio Operator: S/Sgt. C W Barnum – POW
Ball Turrett: Sgt. William J.J. Fiory – POW
Left Waist: Sgt. Joseph H. Palladino – POW
Right Waist: Sgt. Joseph (NMI) Petrillo – POW
Tail Gunner: Sgt. W. G. Zordel – POW

The pilot, 2nd Lt. Thomas R. Francis, probably went to his death, holding the airplane in a steady position so his crew could jump, and he stayed a few seconds longer than he should have. He probably wanted to make sure they were all out. I mention his name here because the name should be remembered.

B-17 SO-M (547th Squadron) Crew:

Pilot: 2nd Lt. Charles W. Baker – POW
Co-Pilot: First Officer Leonard F. Koos – POW
Navigator: 2nd Lt. Phillip L. Carlin – POW
Bombardier: 2nd Lt. William M. Shaner – POW
Top Turret: Sgt. Harry L. Gutierrez – KIA
Radio Operator: S/Sgt. William A. Sneed – POW
Ball Turret: Sgt. Carroll D. Swartzendruber – KIA
Left Waist: S/Sgt. Harry T. Hamilton – POW
Right Waist: Sgt. George (NMI) Sabo – POW
Tail Gunner: Sgt. Salvatore (NMI) Soto – KIA

In a few seconds, 4 men are dead, some of the other crewmen wounded, and the prisoners were in for almost a year of suffering in prison camps. The Generals say that it's a small price to pay for putting the bombs on the target, but the names of Harry I. Gutierrez, Carroll D. Swartzendruber and Salvatore Soto should be enshrined in stone and remembered forever. They were brave young men and they made the ultimate sacrifice.

The Me-109s had darted up through the overcast and fired into the bellies of the B-17s sending them spiraling down trailing smoke and fire. The German fighters had ducked right back into the undercast and disappeared. I told the crew to be alert; our plane being so low in the formation was a natural prey for the fighters. They would be anxious to add to their score, and we looked like easy pickings.

We opened our bomb bay doors, alerted the ball turret gunner to point his guns down and keep his eyes open. I let the copilot fly the airplane, and reached down and grabbed hold of the bailing wire that was threaded back to the toilet stool flush valve. The whole crew was tense, and apprehensive. In about a minute, the ball turret gunner reported on the intercom, "Get ready, here comes one."

My hand tightened on the bailing wire trigger, and regardless of the cold (minus 40 degrees Fahrenheit) I was sweating. The fighter didn't t have to be teased into position. He was climbing, coming at our belly, when the ball turret gunner yelled "Now!"

I immediately jerked the bailing wire, and the ball turret gunner started firing. Out of the corner of my eye I saw a tremendous orange flash and knew the jellied gasoline had been ignited. Looking down, I saw the German fighter with all the fabric burned off the control surfaces and the pilot wiggling the stick wondering what had happened to his control. The bombardier had a beautiful view of the pilot, and he reported there was a puzzled look on his face. As the German fighter fell off on its wing, the pilot bailed out.

The crew was excited and happy, and they all started talking on the intercom at once. I warned them to be quiet and not let down their guard; there were still German fighters in the area. We closed the bomb bay doors and moved back into formation. Being low man in the formation, it was obvious that no one else had seen our downing of the German fighter and I didn't figure we could get a confirmation. As it turned out, two different planes claimed they had shot down a German fighter, and one of them got credit for it.

The ball turret gunner told us that the jellied gasoline had come out perfectly, and he had been quick to ignite it with his tracer fire. The explosion had caused him to lose sight of the German fighter temporarily, but he also had seen the plane with its scorched skin and the fabric burned off the control surfaces. He said the control surfaces were being rapidly moved in every direction as the pilot wiggled the stick, wondering what had happened.

Back at the base, we didn't talk much about it. The crew chief of the airplane was aware of what we were doing, and a few other enlisted men were privy to our secret. After we had gotten our third enemy fighter, our crew chief painted three small toilets up under the pilot's window. They were not prominent, but they could be seen from the ground. We were elated at our success, and were very proud of the fact that we burned off the control surfaces of the German fighters, and down they went with a puzzled pilot wiggling the stick around, wondering why he didn't have control of the airplane.

The West Pointers on the base were not aware of our success, and we thought they would probably frown at our method of delivering the lethal dose of jellied gasoline. However the secret was getting harder and harder to contain. Most of the enlisted men on the base knew about our toilet, and thought it a pretty good joke.

In a couple of weeks we had our fifth enemy fighter down. We had five, which entitled us to call ourselves the Ace Crew, but the bloom was off the rose, and I was called to Headquarters to see the Commanding Officer. I expected a warm welcome, and congratulations, but instead I got my ass chewed out. He ordered me to take the toilet stool out of the bomb bay, and in no uncertain terms told me that I was a disgrace to the Army Air Corps Officers Corp. I was a disgrace to all the officers, who faithfully served, followed orders, used Government equipment that was issued to fight the Hun and did not embarrass the Commanding Officer. "That was my toilet your crew took. I've had to use the regular officers' latrine." His face was red and his eyes were bulging. "What if the General heard about this, fighting the enemy with a toilet stool," he shouted. "He probably would have my gawd damn eagles."

I was crestfallen, but the crew and I quickly took out the bailing wire trigger, and put the plane back in shape to fight the Hun in a more conventional manner. The tall old Colonel got his revenge. He must have been amused while he signed the order to give me the DEATH SENTENCE. He had given me an extra combat mission, (not the crew), and I flew 31 instead 30 missions.

The Toilet Stool Ace, 1999

CHARLIE BROWN AND THE GOOD GERMAN

How cool is this!?

Charlie Brown was a B-17 Flying Fortress pilot with the 379th Bomber Group at Kimbolton, England. His B-17 was called "Ye old Pub" and was in a terrible state, having been hit by flak and fighters. The compass was damaged and they were flying deeper over enemy territory instead of heading home to Kimbolton. After flying over an enemy airfield, a pilot named Franz Steigler was ordered to take off and shoot down the B-17. When he got near the B-17, he could not believe his eyes. In his words, he "Had never seen a plane in such a bad state." The tail and rear section were severely damaged, and the tail gunner wounded. The top gunner was all over the top of the fuselage. The nose was smashed and there were holes everywhere.

Despite having ammunition, Franz flew to the side of the B-17 and looked at Charlie Brown. Brown was scared and struggling to control his damaged and blood-stained plane.

Aware that they had no idea where they were going, Franz waved at Charlie to turn 180 degrees. Franz escorted and guided the stricken plane to slightly over the North Sea towards England. He then saluted Charlie Brown and turned away, back to Europe. When Franz landed he told the c/o that the plane had been shot down over the sea, and never told the truth to anybody. Charlie Brown and the remains of his crew told all at the briefing, but were ordered never to talk about it. More than 40 years later, Charlie Brown wanted to find the Luftwaffe pilot who saved the crew. After years of research, Franz was found. He had never talked about the incident, not even at post-war reunions. They met in the USA at a 379th Bomber Group reunion, together with 25 people who are alive now—all because Franz never fired his guns that day.

Research shows that Charlie Brown lived in Seattle and Franz Siegler had moved to Vancouver, BC after the war. When they finally met, they had lived less than 200 miles apart for the past 50 years!

COMMANDING GENERAL

MAJ. GEN. NATHAN F. TWINING

Bomb Load

15th AAF, Nov. 1 — During the first year of its operation from bases in Italy, the 15th AAF dropped 210,000 tons of bombs on enemy and enemy-held territory. During the same period, 15th AAF gunners expended 30,000,000 rounds of small caliber ammunition.

A convoy of trucks carrying 210,000 tons of bombs would stretch 5,600 miles, on the basis of 15 trucks per mile. Placed end to end, 30,000,000 bullets would make an unbroken line from New York to California. In weight, such an amount of bullets is equal to 2,500 average size passenger automobiles.

Meat For A Month: 12 Thousand Cattle

15th AAF, Nov. 1—In a month's time, the 15th Air Force and Service Command is issued enough food rations to feed the city of Muncie, Ind., (population 56,000) for two years.

The issue of fresh meat alone for the month of October was equivalent to 12,000 head of cattle. During the summer, 15th AAF organizations made and consumed 40,000 gallons of ice cream, using 8,400 tons of ice to freeze it. That amount of ice cream would fill a Muncie drug store's requirements for four years.

INTERESTING AIR FORCE STATISTICS

Read the information next to the photograph. It vividly illustrates the enormous number of supplies and products it took to maintain an Air Force Command…a logistical nightmare.

GENERAL NATHAN F. TWINING

This picture was taken and reported in 1944. Years later, August 15, 1957, as a four star general, he was made chairman of the Joint Chiefs of Staff by President Eisenhower. He commanded the 20th Air Force when the Enola Gay dropped the atomic bomb on Hiroshima.

CORPORAL AND MRS WARREN JENSEN
TAKE OTTO NORGAARD TO D.C

SUN, BALTIMORE, TUESDAY, MARCH 2, 1954

CORPORAL WARREN JENSEN

Fallon To Stay In Hospital For Time

[Special to The Boston Sun]

OTTO NORGAARD   MRS. JOAN JENSEN

Mr. Norgaard Goes To D.C.; Pistol Shots Salute Him

Corporal and Mrs. Warren Jensen took Mrs. Jensen's father, Otto Norgaard, on a visit from Minnesota to Washington, yesterday for his first look at the nation's Capitol.

[Continued On Page 20, Column 3]

Legion Sponsors Speaking Test

91ST BOMB GROUP (H)

The 322nd Dailies

Daily Reports from the 322nd Bomb Squadron
SUBMITTED BY FRANK FARR:

From our viewpoint today, the Second World War was a black-and-white pageant of men and machines battling across or above a grainy, forgotten landscape.

War is a narrative voiced by calm, analytical announcers who examine the past from an academic distance. Often forgotten is the work of tens of thousands of non-combatant clerks and record keepers whose jobs were to capture on paper the administrative minutia of the process of war.

Their efforts, while doubtless tedious at the time, provide an outstanding backdrop against which the war plays out in practical terms. It is the "how" behind the "when" and "where".

The Daily Reports from the 322nd Bomb Squadron is part of that vast store of administrative detail. They are the actual day-to-day records of the squadrons missions and movements from the inception of the group through the end of the war.

This record is a valuable resource in many ways. For veterans, they can augment memories with hard facts. For researchers they provide solid dates around which to base further investigation. Children and grandchildren of the 322nd veterans will be able to pinpoint where their family members were at any given time.

Many thanks to:

Frank Farr, who transcribed this information for the 91st Bomb Group Website.

This information was found at the web site of the 91st Bomb Group.

I took the liberty and privilege to include these three pages from it. They vividly depict what these brave young men experienced in the air war that was of such vital importance to the defeat of Germany.

Often we infantrymen would look up after hearing the drone of their engines as they flew in formation toward their target. Contrails usually followed the engines. Even though we were miserable, dirty and worn out, we did not envy any of them. We could not imagine the courage it took to be up there flying and being subjected to enemy fighters and anti-aircraft guns pounding away at you. We saluted and prayed for them. THANK YOU, Charles Pefinis, Editor

44-322 Dailies of the 91ˢᵗ BG   **Pages 4-5 of 128**

One Me109 destroyed by S/S Robert N. Clark, BTG 070

Losses: Crews of 2nd Lt. Page, A/C 076, and 2nd Lt Murdoch, A/C057, failed to return.

HEADQUARTERS
EUROPEAN THEATRE OF OPERATIONS
UNITED STATES ARMY
IMMEDIATE RELEASE

16 JANUARY 1944
NUMBER 8274
FORTRESS CREW BAGS 10 FIGHTERS, RETURNS FROM OSCHERSLEBEN AT TREE-TOP LEVEL

Coming back from Oschersleben on two engines, a bullet-ridden U.S. Eighth AAF flying fortress piloted by 1st Lt. Eldridged V. Greer, 29, of Houston, Texas, roared down the main streets of German towns, used trees as cover from pursuing enemy aircraft as it sped along at sometimes less than tree-top eight, strafed German soldiers on the ground, and finally crossed the enemy coast so low that Lt. Greer said, "The flak towers had to shoot down at us."

The fortress was the "Spirit of '44," and its crew claimed a bag of ten enemy fighters during the great Eighth AAF attack on the German fighter plant at Oschersleben last Tuesday.

When the ship landed in England its nose had been shot out, cannon shells had blown gaping holes in its wings and fuselage, and it was riddled from tail to nose with bullet holes, but none of the crew members were injured.

In a mad race that lasted about an hour and one-half, the fort was pursued by two twin-engineD German planes for more than 200 miles. Lt. Greer alternately dived, climbed, and then dived again to skim along the ground, barely avoiding electric high-tension lines and other ground installations.

"Wherever possible, we would fly below tree-top level alongside a wooded area," said the pilot. "Every time we saw a village, we'd pull over and fly down the streets so the fighters would have to shoot into their own town to shoot at us."

Three times the exhausted crew prepared for a crash landing inside enemy territory. The bombardier smashed his precious bomb-sight. The gunners took off flying boots and put on field shoes and divided up their cigarettes. But the "Spirit of '44" kept on going on its two remaining engines, with the enemy still chasing it. At one point they passed 25 feet above the crashed wreckage of another Fort, and the tail gunner, S/Sgt Robert A. Mueller, of Woodridge, N.J., strafed and killed a German soldier guarding the crashed Fort.

On the way to Oschersleben, "The Spirit of '44" has participated in what was probably the greatest air battle in history. German bombers flew at the bomber formations 25 at a time, firing everything they had. The bombardier on "The Spirit of '44", Lt. Louie R. Dobbs, of Katemacy, Texas, fired the new fortress chin turret throughout the battle and claimed the destruction of three Focke-Wulfe 190s. One was seen to crash, another exploded shortly after going into a dive, and the third disintegrated completely in the air.

Tech. Sgt. Casmer W. Lewkowski, top turret gunner from Peninsula, Ohio, also claimed three enemy planes. Sgt. Mueller, the tail gunner, destroyed two.

The ball turret gunner, S/Sgt. Ernest J. Koger, Jr., of Eau Claire, Wis., claimed one FW-190. When he reached England, he found three holes the size of baseballs in his ball turret, but he miraculously had escaped injury.

The crew's tenth fighter was claimed by S/Sgt. James E. Purton, waist gunner, from East Liverpool, Ohio.

"Over the target we lost the engines and our oxygen system," related 2nd Lt. William D. Wood, of Pleasure Ville, Ky., the co-pilot. "We dropped down on the deck, fighting all the way down, to begin the race with the two Messerschmitt that picked us up deep in Germany and stayed with us to the coast. Between attacks they flew along like a friendly escort, one on each side of us, about 1,000 yards away.

"When we landed in England, we had about 250 bullet holes criss-crossed all through the ship. The plastic nose was shot out; there was a hole 18 inches in diameter in the radio room; a 20 mm. shell had exploded in the wings; and the bomb bay doors, which had been hit over the target, were part-way open."

S/Sgt. Mueller, the tail gunner, declared, "I'm proud to be on that crew. The fellows all used their heads. If we had any pilot other than Lt. Greer, we probably never would have got home. As a matter of fact, I can't believe I'm home now."

Other members of the crew were: 2nd Lt. Marvin D. Anderson, navigator, of Kansas City, Mo.,; T/Sgt. Garner Walters, radio operator, Broadway, N.J.; S/Sgt. Woodrow Wade, waist gunner, Henderson, Tex.

http://www.91stbombgroup.com/Dailies/322nd1944.html

GARY GOLDMAN'S FATHER

SUBMITTED BY GARY GOLDMAN:

Gary Goldman is a new friend. His father was a physician during WWII. He was with the Medical Detachment 261st Field Artillery Battalion. He served in England and in Germany from the fall of 1944 to 1945.

Gary has graciously allowed us to include two letters that his father wrote to Gary's grandfather. They are unique to this era because they are V-Mail letters. V-mail letters were prints of microfilm negatives. This was a great idea because thousands of letters could be recorded this way and transported easily with a minimum of bulk. My family sent me letters using regular envelope and paper. All my letters to my family came to it via USPS but on V-mail "letter" paper.

C. Pefinis

c/o Postmaster New York
N.Y.

30th Oct. '44
[Date]

In a small Town on the coast of England.

(I) It's true what a friend of mine said about England. He had complained about the cold peculiarly penetrating night air. I too, (I blush to say it) sleep in long woolen underwear and socks, a woolen sweater and 4 blankets and keep wondering how the cold manages to get thru. But feeling is believing. Nothing like New Orleans (Remember?). Much better now, however. Just bought an electric heater! Mmmm-m-m, much more like it. It is still difficult to realize I'm here. Things are so different I feel as if I'm twins; one of me standing afar off and acting as a sort of commentator. I guess it sounds rather vague and silly but it was a kind of magic-carpet transition from practically the gulf of Mexico to chilly England. The native expressions intrigue me. I've learned to say cinema for movie (incidentally smoking is permitted throut the house and balcony seats cost more than those downstairs), wireless for radio, torch for flashlight, que for line, pub for saloon, chips for Frenchfried potatoes, and of course, cheerio. The kids here love gum. They often approach you with the now familiar "gum, chum?" The stuff being rather tightly rationed to us, my answer is too often, "no".

(III) I've visited New York's rival. The historic and proclaimed landmarks of London thrilled me. London at war stirred me a strange mixture of resentment, pity and deep admiration. Resentment at the wanton destruction of which man is capable, pity for the ones that must have suffered terrible physical & mental anguish in the memento of ruins left spotting the city, and admiration for the uncomplaining manner in which the survivors are working and carrying on. The orderliness & cleanliness under the circumstances is amazing. I visited Westminster abbey whose 1200 years of antiquity compels a silent, oppressive awe upon those passing thru it. The halls seem to echo the whisperings of famed personages departed centuries ago and who lie under the very stone blocks one walks upon and in the walls one brushes by. Just to jostle you rudely back to the present how is etc. & other things more personal

V···−MAIL

POST OFFICE DEPARTMENT PERMIT NO. 17

The city at night is completely blacked out, but the darkness still throbs with the sounds of people & taxis and buses who find their way around heaven knows how.

No._____

To

From

_____
(Sender's name)

_____
(Sender's address)

A. Goldman

(CENSOR'S STAMP)

28 January 1945
(Date)

Dear Dad,
Germany

I'm tired, and it's 45 minutes past midnight, but I can't go to sleep without writing you. Today I haven't written you since January 14th, but, believe me, I was kept on the go. Today I received your letter, the one you sent out January the 12th, and I was surprised, but happy to learn you have found some one you would like to share your future with. I am certain the choice you have made, Dad, is wise, and I wish you and my new Mother the blessings of many, many years of companionship, harmony, and happiness. May she helps brighten your life and, by the reflected light of unselfishness, brighten her own devotion brighten her own. I shall always regret being absent from the ceremony but war plays cruel tricks. Please tell me about her. I am naturally very much interested.

As I write, the given stove in my temporary concrete and brick cellar "home" is refusing to function smoothly for an American and has decided to give out gobs of smoke. I can't open the small window now because that would break the black out. As soon as I finish this letter I'll put out the light and open the "joint" for ventilation. Tonight the moon is full and golden and bright. It lights up a scene of ruin made beautiful by the soft white blanket of snow. The guns have been rather quiet practically fairly silent for rather long stretches this evening as if they too want to add to the peacefulness of the night scene.

If I can get into Belgium or Holland in the near future I will see if I can find a gift I would like to send (?) Germany so battered, not many civilians, etc.

V···-MAIL

☆ U. S. GOVERNMENT PRINTING OFFICE | 1945 16—28143-4

about the $260 and about allotment coming in Feb. for Jan. — good conduct pass

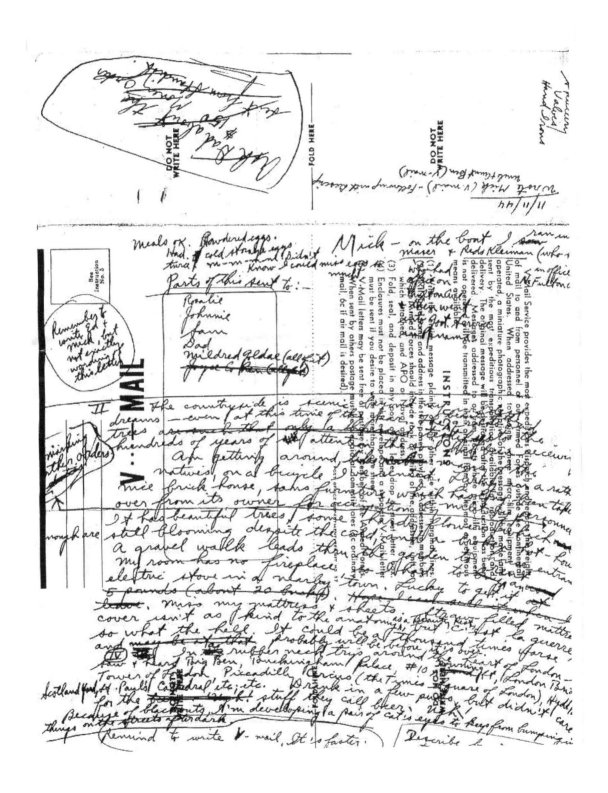

ODDBALL HISTORICAL INFORMATION ABOUT WWII

SUBMITTED BY COL. D.C. SWINEFORD, USMC, Ret., HISTORY BUFF

The first German serviceman killed in WW II was killed by the Japanese (China, 1937; the first American serviceman killed was killed by the Russians (England, 1940); the highest ranking American killed was Lt. Gen. Lesley McNair, killed by the US Army Air Corps…So much for allies.

The youngest US Serviceman was 12-year-old Calvin Graham, USN. He was wounded and given a Dishonorable Discharge for lying about his age. His benefits were later restored by an act of Congress.

At the time of Pearl Harbor the top US Navy command was called the CINCUS (pronounced "sink us"); the shoulder patch of the US Army's 45th Infantry division was the Swastika; and Hitler's private train was named "Amerika." All three were soon changed for PR purposes.

More US servicemen died in the Air Corps than the Marine Corps. While completing the required 25 missions your chance of being killed was 71%.

Generally speaking, there was no such thing as an average fighter pilot. You were either an ace or a target. For instance, Japanese ace Hiroyoshi Nishizawa shot down over 80 fighter planes. He died while a passenger on a cargo plane.

It was common practice on fighter planes to load every fifth round with a tracer round to aid in aiming. This was a mistake. Tracers had different ballistics so (at long range) if your tracers were hitting the target, 80% of your rounds were missing. Worse yet, tracers instantly told your enemy he was under fire and from which direction. Worst of all was the practice of loading a string of tracers at the end of the belt to tell you that you were out of ammo. This was definitely not something you wanted to tell the enemy. Units that stopped using tracers saw their success rate nearly double and their loss rate go down.

YOU'VE GOT TO LOVE THIS ONE…

When Allied armies reached the Rhine the first thing the men did was pee in it. This was pretty universal from the lowest private to Winston Churchill (who made a big show of it) and General Patton (who had himself photographed while in the act).

German ME-264 bombers were capable of bombing New York City but it wasn't worth the effort.

German submarine U-120 was sunk by a malfunctioning toilet.

Among the first "Germans captured at Normandy were several Koreans. They had been forced to fight for the Japanese Army until they were captured by the Russians and forced to fight for the Russian Army until they were captured by the Germans and forced to fight for the German Army until they were captured by the US Army.

AND THE BEST FOR LAST…

Following a massive naval bombardment, 35,000 US and Canadian troops stormed ashore at Kiska, in the Aleutian Islands. Twenty-one troops were killed in the firefight. It would have been worse if there had been any Japanese on the island.

TAPS

If any of you have ever been to a military funeral where taps were played, this comment provides a new meaning and insight.

We in the United States have all heard the haunting tune, "Taps." It's the song that gives us a lump in our throats, and brings tears to our eyes. Most of us, though, do not know the story behind this melody.

Reportedly, it all began in 1862 during the Civil War, when Union Army Captain Robert Ellicombe was with his men near Harrison's Landing in Virginia. The Confederate Army was on the other side of the narrow strip of land. During the night, Captain Ellicombe heard the moans of a soldier who lay wounded on the field. Not knowing if it was a Union or Confederate soldier, the Captain decided to risk his life and bring the stricken man back for medical attention.

Crawling on his stomach through the gunfire, the Captain reached the stricken soldier and began pulling him toward his encampment. When the Captain finally reached his own lines, he discovered it was a Confederate soldier, but he had died. The Captain lit a lantern, he suddenly caught his breath and went numb with shock. In the dim light, he saw the face of the soldier. It was his own son. The boy had been studying music in the South when the war broke out. Without telling his father, the boy enlisted in the Confederate Army.

The following morning, heartbroken, the father asked permission of his superiors to give his son a full military burial, despite his enemy status. His request was only partially granted. The captain had asked if he could have a group of Army band members play a funeral dirge for the funeral. The request was denied since the soldier was a Confederate. But, out of respect for the father, they allowed him the services of one musician.

The Captain chose a bugler. He asked him to play a series of musical notes that he had found on a piece of paper in the pocket of his son's uniform. This wish was granted.

The haunting melody, we now know as "Taps"…used at military funerals was born.

HERE ARE THESE CHERISHED WORDS:

Day is done…
Gone the sun…
From the lakes…
From the hills…
From the sky…
All is well…
Safely rest…
God is nigh…
Fading light…
Dims the sight…
And a star…
Gems the sky…
Gleaming bright…
From afar…
Drawing nigh…
Falls the night…
Thanks and praise…
For our days…
Neath the sun…
Neath the stars…
Neath the sky…
As we go…
This we know…
God is nigh…

I too have felt the chills while listening to "Taps" but I never knew there were words to it. I now have an even deeper respect and feel an intense sorrow remembering those lost while serving our nation.

"Taps" should also serve as a reminder of the sacrifice and courage exhibited each day by our servicemen and women as they perform their duties throughout the world.

Unfortunately the above is folk lore, but I love it. I first heard that version as a ROTC cadet at Tech High School in Atlanta in the early 1940's. We assumed it was true.

I chose to include it because, notwithstanding its source, it was considered by many as authentic and brought forth those emotions appropriate to the occasion.

As I considered its inclusion, I checked the internet hoping it was accurate. Sadly it was not. Yet for many of us for 60+ years, it was authentic. I'll leave it at that. Here is what Snopes (http:www.snopes.com) says. Charles Pefinis

Then as now, 'Taps' serves as a vital component in ceremonies honoring military dead. It is also understood by American servicemen as an end-of-day 'lights out' signal.

When "Taps" is played at a military funeral, it is customary to salute if in uniform, or place your hand over your heart if not.

Origins: It's hard to feel surprised when a melody as hauntingly beautiful as Taps picks up a legend about how it came to be written -- it's too mournfully direct a piece for the mere truth to suffice.

Taps was composed in July 1862 at Harrison's Landing in Virginia, but after that the fanciful e-mail quoted above parts

way with reality. There was no dead son, Confederate or otherwise; no lone bugler sounding out the dead boy's last composition. How the call came into being was never anything more than one influential soldier deciding his unit could use a bugle call for particular occasions and setting about to come up with one.

If anyone can be said to have composed 'Taps,' it was Brig. Gen. Daniel Butterfield, Commander of the 3rd Brigade, 1st Division, V Army Corps, Army of the Potomac, during the American Civil War. Dissatisfied with the customary firing of three rifle volleys at the conclusion of burials during battle and also needing a method of ceremonially imparting meaning to the end of a soldier's day, he likely altered an older piece known as "Tattoo," a French bugle call used to signal "lights out," into the call we now know as 'Taps.' (Alternatively, he wrote the whole thing from scratch, a possibility not at all supported by his lack of musical background and ability.)

Whether he wrote it straight from the cuff or improvised something new by rearranging an older work, Butterfield brought 'Taps' into being. With the help of his bugler, Oliver W. Norton of Chicago, the concept was transformed into its present form. "Taps" was quickly taken up by both sides of the conflict, and within months was being sounded by buglers in both Union and Confederate forces.

ANOTHER VERSION OF THE ORIGIN OF "TAPS"

A tune sounded during ceremonies at the Tomb of the Unknowns
and at military funerals everywhere is known simply as ...Taps

by Kathryn Shenkle*

During a visit to Arlington National Cemetery, Va., you might hear the echoes of "Taps" being sounded by a bugler from one of the armed forces of the United States.

The 132-year-old bugle call was composed by Brig. Gen. Daniel Butterfield, who commanded the 3rd Brigade, 1st Division, V Army Corps, Army of the Potomac, during the American Civil War.

Butterfield wrote "Taps" at Harrison's Landing, Va., in July 1862 to replace the customary firing of three rifle volleys at the end of burials during battle. "Taps" also replaced "Tatoo," the French bugle call to signal "lights out." Butterfield's bugler, Oliver W. Norton of Chicago, was the first to sound the new call. Within months, "Taps" was sounded by buglers in both Union and Confederate forces.

"Taps" concludes nearly 15 military funerals conducted with honors each weekday at the Arlington National Cemetery as well as hundreds of others around the country. The tune is also played at many memorial services in Arlington's Memorial Amphitheater and at gravesites throughout the cemetery.

"Taps" is sounded during the 2,500 military wreath ceremonies conducted at the Tomb of the Unknowns every year, including the ones to be held this Memorial Day. The ceremonies are viewed by many groups, including veterans, schools, and foreign officials.

One of the final bugle calls of the day on military installations, "Taps" is played at 10 p.m. as a signal to service members that it is "lights out."

When "Taps" is played, it is customary to salute, if in uniform, or place your hand over your heart if not. The composer of "Taps" was born Oct. 31, 1831, in Utica, N.Y., and joined the Army in Washington, D.C.

He was awarded the Medal of Honor in the U.S. Volunteers on June 27, 1862. After his brigade lost more than 600 men in the Battle of Gaines Mill,

Butterfield took up the colors of the 83rd Pennsylvania Volunteers. Under heavy enemy fire, he encouraged the depleted ranks to regroup and continue the battle.

Butterfield died July 17, 1901, and was buried at the U.S. Military Academy at West Point, N.Y. "Taps" was sounded at his funeral.

- Article reprinted with permission from Kathryn Shenkle, Historian with Arlington National Cemetery.

AN 87TH INFANTRYMAN GOING THRU THE GERMAN TOWN OF BERTOLE

MARCH 17TH 1945 THE BEGINNING OF THE CAPTURE OF KOBLENZ

THE 87ᵀᴴ CROSSING THE RHINE RIVER MARCH 25, 1945

After the Bombing the Doughboys March Into Ruined Plauen, Germany

I took these pictures using a camera I found in a house in Koblenze
or what was was left of it.In the camera was a roll of film which had
be used. The pictures of the German soldiers that appear here was those
in the exposed film. .

I do not know the name of the city pictured, but because of its apparent size,
it could have been Koblenze or Plauen.

Surrendering German general at Plauen.

Boarding LCI, Le Havre, France

More boarding

The USS West Point, the ship that brought us home.

HOME AT LAST!

A 30 DAY FURLOUGH THEN.............................
TO FORT BENNING TO TRAIN FOR
THE INVASION OF JAPAN!!!!! DAMN!

The USS America, massive, still a troop ship, sailed majestically into New York's harbor. Geysers of water sprayed into the air from dozens of fire boats. The low eerie sound of fog horns was deafening. The thought occurred to me that with all the men hanging on the port side it would lean that way. Foolish me. It was one humongous vessel. No chance!

Disembarking was chaotic. We wrestled with our duffel bags filled with everything we owned. (Mine also contained two German rifles.) I could not believe the number of people screaming the names of some of the guys, who were yelling back to them. I marveled that that knew when we were coming and on this ship!

Herded into a warehouse structure, we formed in groups of our organizations, then headed to the railroad yard. Chaos reigned!

But it worked, magically.

I boarded the train. I was on my way home!

Sitting at a window seat looking out as row after row of homes built right next to the track went whizzing by I wondered how these people lived. All that racket, how do they survive this noise day-in-day-out.

When I awoke, we were North Carolina; the clacking sound of the train wheels was soothing. Damn, in a few hours I'd be in Georgia! Finally! As we entered the suburbs of Atlanta, memories flooded my mind. Many times past I had been there but had not SEEN these homes and stores and traffic. Now I saw them clearly. It seemed I had been gone for years and years. Very vivid!

The train tracks go right through the city running south. As we approached Fort McPherson, I was shocked to observe a gang of German soldiers tilling the land of a farm! They were probably POW's captured during the North African campaign. That was common during the early days of the conflict. What better place to "store" prisoners of war than a place 3000 miles away.

Fort Mac was about 20 miles from our home in Druid Hills (remember the movie, "Driving Ms Daisy", the same neighborhood). A call to my parents – Hey folks, I'm home – caused a panic at the Pefinis household. Who was going to come get me? My father and my uncle Nick were on the road somewhere marketing Burger Beer. There was no car at the house.

I told mom (who was so excited, in tears and screaming, "Kostakee mou! Kostakee mou! Efxaristo ton THEO pou se efere peeso!"[(My (child) Kosta! My (child) Kosta!.I thank GOD for bringing you back!] . . that I'd figure a way back, maybe take a cab.

I sauntered over to headquarters to find my cousin Victor. He was still in the typing pool. (Vic was my co-conspirator in my infamous-going-home-for-Thanksgiving dinner two years before . . . . . my one and only AWOL event!)

Now again, two plus years later, my cuz and I drive to my home this time located at 935 Springdale Dr. Mom went nuts! She was jumping up and down laughing, crying, hugging us both . . .out of her mind!

I was stunned, awed at this house. While I was gone my family had re-located to this magnificent house, so very different from our tiny (800 sq.ft) house on Cooper Street which was only about 2 miles from downtown Atlanta. This one was North and about 10 miles from downtown. It was a mansion, over 3000 square feet. The cost was $10,000. (Now worth according to Zillow, $1,038,500! Damn!)

A thirty day furlough! WOW! Wonderful, but, boy, did those days go by fast.

My papers stated that on August 5th, 1945 I was to report to Fort Mac to get further orders. So, I went out there. I sat with a bunch of other guys in a room which looked like a very small auditorium with elevated seats. The Sarge in charge would read names of men who would then walk down the aisle to receive their orders. My name was not called. So I went home. The next day the same thing, no name read, I went home! This went on for a solid week! Man, I was elated. (What was going on was that God again to my assistance. Really!)

Some of the personnel files had somehow gotten misplaced. We were required to go out to Fort Mac each day to report in and wait there to hear our names called out to be sent to Fort Benning where the 87th was now located to begin training for the invasion of Japan.

There were four of us all whose name started with the letter "P". After a couple of days I noticed that and figured what had happened. I kept my mouth shut. One guy Pittman was getting antsy and kept wondering out loud about not going to Benning – dumb ass. I told him to cool it. Finally after about a week he goes to the Sarge in charge and COMPLAINS! That did it. They found them!

Now at Fort Benning we were assumed to be AWOL (All my close friends thought that I had lost it!) Me - AWOL legally? Two years before I was AWOL but not "legally". I guess what goes around does come around!

Then Hiroshima and Nagasaki happened! It is over!! Thank GOD!! No invasion of Japan!! The 87th Infantry Division was to be one of the first divisions to front "Operation Downfall", its code name.

For the next 8 months I was stationed at good ol' Fort Mac again. My job was to help in processing the men being discharged, to specifically explain their insurance (forgot which and why) and then painfully to assist in a goodbye program to the tune of (sickening to me) Hawaiian music. I had the enviable job of adding and removing the phonograph records. When my turn came for this torture, I gave them my record of "In The Mood" to be played. Perfect eh?

Now one more choice piece to this fascinating account of ol'"Piff" being discharged. At the end of the counter line (similar to a cafeteria line) that we were required to walk was a handsome, strong-looking, top sergeant (could have been a movie star) who with disarming charm held a pen at ready saying something like, "Well, MR. Pefinis, sounds good doesn't it, Mister! Sign right here. This will make you quite a few bucks a month and even a retirement amount in about 20 years. It allows you to join the Reserves. You spend a couple of weeks in the summer at a camp, lotta fun. Sign right here".

I thought I was experiencing a nightmare. "Now let me understand this. You want me to sign something so that I can have more of the same crap that I have lived with for 30 months?? No sir, Sarge. Not me, no way! "

Jim Panagos is as old neighborhood friend of mine. We grew up together. Jim too served as a combat infantryman in Belgium and Germany. (When his company was crossing the Rhine, his boat capsized. Jim fell like a rock straight down weighted by 80 pounds of stuff. But the good Lord saved him too. Going down his legs STRADDLED a cable of some sort. So Jim "walked" his way hand-over-hand to the shore!)

Well ol' Jim fell for the spiel of the Reserves guy as he got his discharge. He signed on the dotted line. He would make a few bucks each month; go to camp for a couple of weeks each year and get a pension after 20 years .. Lovely!

Ol' Jim never figured on Korea happening. But it did! Being smart, he had attained the rank of a Lieutenant. Now Lieutenant Panagos was slated to lead an infantry platoon against the hordes of Korean and Chinese soldiers in frozen Korea! "WOW! Damn! I never figured on THIS" went thru ol' Jim's mind. Poor Jim liked to have died!

We pulled all the political strings we had. It worked. We managed to get him transferred to Military Intelligence and domiciled in the good ol' USA!

May 1st, 1946, I am out of the Army!

This time my parents are waiting for me at Fort Mac's gate. My two sisters were jammed in the car, too. That massive duffel bag still containing two German rifles was stuffed in the trunk. As Dad drove away, I opened that manila envelope to look again and show my folks that gorgeous Honorable Discharge Certificate. I also looked at the "Separation Qualification Record" stapled to the Discharge. Yes, it was there. It was a tiny "s" which had been typed smack in the center of the wreath above the head of the American Eagle which adorned the "SEPARATION QUALIFICATION RECORD" (a document which always accompanied the Discharge papers). It was typed by a lovely young lady, Sarah Moreland. Sarah was very sweet to all the returning combat veterans, She'd bake a cake and bring into the office. Her job was typing all the discharge papers. Great gal!

I entered Georgia Tech that September under the GI Bill – best thing that ever happened to me. Graduated with a degree in Industrial Management in June of 1949.

Finally, as with most veterans of WWII, what we experienced was monumental, a life changing event. Though many times it was painful beyond description, yet to a man, I have never heard of a veteran that regretted his service or what he endured. It was a true honor to serve and fight for our country, the greatest in the world.

Today, as an 84 year old, I salute my friends that survive and mourn those who have passed on. But as with all combat veterans, we applaud with awe the men and women that served in Korea, the Viet Nam war, the Gulf war and especially those now in Iraq and Afghanistan who are protecting our

Nation. We <u>SALUTE YOU,</u> men and women, for your dedication and for your love of freedom for our country!!

CHRISTINE NIKAS...A TRIBUTE TO A SUPERB YOUNG LADY!

"God bless America" has been the running theme in our hearts and our minds these last few weeks prior to Memorial Day and the dedication of the Memorial to WWII veterans.

Evidence of the depth and the love our children have for our country is not always obvious. At times, a child in the innocence of youth can be truly eloquent and very telling.

What will follow relates to Christine Nikas, the daughter of Basil and Penny Nikas of Bethesda, MD, great friends of ours.

Christine, a fifth grader at a Bethesda, Maryland school, questioned me about my service in World War II as a combat infantryman. Her class had a project studying this War of Wars. I was a person with whom she could communicate to learn something about it. Being unable to coordinate a visit to her school, I chose to send pictures of myself and members of our squad and other photos of interest taken during the war.

What I received back is a testament of this child's beautiful intellect, eloquence and tender heart.

The Statement and the Poem along with the photographs were beautifully arranged, framed behind glass, and given to me as a token of friendship.

I treasure them as one of the finest gifts I have ever received.

Charles G. Pefinis
Publisher: Pefinis-Matheson Theme Books
www.howwewonthewar.com

Dear Mr. Pefinis,
War Veteran

I am a student at Westbrook Elementary School. My fifth grade class just finished learning about World War II and we also read about the Valentine's for Veterans program. Since we had just learned about veterans and saw the amazing photographs you brought back from the war, I decided it would be nice to send a Valentine to you because we learned what you have gone through. I am also sending a poem that I wrote about WWII.

I hope that you liked this poem that I wrote in my class. I will conclude my letter by wishing you a very happy Valentine's Day, and thank you for serving our country in a war.

Sincerely
Christine Nikas

87th Infantry Division Association
Ardennes * Rhineland * Central Europe

War
Anger, that fire inside you, the fury of everything that's happening.
Dispute is that quarrel, so colossal, everyone denying that they are wrong.
Fear, it gives you boldness and courage at unexpected times.
Battle is dreadful for the soldiers, and unexpectedly, the family waiting.
Killing is so insane, but in war it seems to be part of your life.
Destruction is what happened in the bombing of Pearl Harbor, so cruel.
Concentration camps come packaged with hate so much, its disgusting.
Hatred is what war is, so full of fierceness, inside everyone.
Suffering happens to everyone, during and after the war.
Suffering, you feel it when you're family member dies.
War is the cause for innocent children to be killed, everyone suffers.

Christine Nikas

THE GI BILL FOR SERVING YOUR COUNTRY!

I was still in the service in 1946 assigned at Fort McPherson, Georgia as a clerk (MOS 055). My home town in Atlanta's Druid Hills section, Springdale road, was only a 25 minute ride from there. I'd get home almost every week end.

Dinners were a joyful occasion at the Pefinis household. My uncle lived with us as part of our family.

One Sunday, a beautiful spring afternoon, with all of us there, uncle, sisters... everybody..., my dad got up from the table for a moment and went into the kitchen. When he returned, he was holding a copy of the Atlanta Journal. He slowly held it, moving it so that each person could read the headline.

In large letters it announced "GI BILL FOR VETERANS"! The article stated that the government had decreed that all veterans would receive a free four year college education including a monthly stipend for having served in the armed services – the G.I.Bill. I was stunned and elated!

Now understand that my father, uncle and mother had all immigrated in the early 1900's to the United States from Greece. Under the Ottoman Empire, Turkey had subjugated Greece for 400 years. Greece finally achieved its independence in 1821. In all those 400 years, there were many attempts to break this yoke of tyranny.

Upon reading this announcement, both my father and uncle said (almost in unison), "Why are they doing this?" I responded, "What do you mean?" My fathers answer, "Why are they rewarding you for fighting for your country? It's your duty to fight for your country!"

Think about that for a moment. "Why are they rewarding you for fighting for your country?" What an apt question for today's society.

Can any one of us imagine being under the rule of a tyrannical regime, e.g. Sadam Hussein, from 1609 to the present? It is no wonder they made that comment!

(FYI, both my father and uncle with no education, used their "sweat equity"' plus the opportunities and freedom offered by this country to lead successful, happy lives.)

Made in the USA
Lexington, KY
16 August 2014